MW00618427

Foreward

A great man once said "Every successful person I've ever known has possessed passion and vision; but, not every person with passion and vision becomes a success."

If only we could all have a perfect world with perfect opportunities to achieve our dreams life. That would indeed be beautiful. Every person would have the power, the ability to control their circumstances, and the capacity to control their destiny. Unfortunately, life is going to throw us curves that we will not be able to catch and some situations that we may not be able to navigate around; yet we still have a choice to make it or succumb to our misfortune. Why? Because "excuses" are an easy way out, an easy explanation of why we do not or could not reach our full potential. Those excuses for incompletion span a wide spectrum:

Time

Money

Opportunity

Childhood

Talent

Bad Luck

Just one excuse after another...but as the author of this book writes, "I Had Every Excuse to Fail, but I Chose None."

As much as any professional work I have ever read, I am certain that this book comes from the heart of a man grounded and rooted in Jeremiah 29:11 "For I know the plans I have for you," declares the LORD, "plans to prosper you and not to harm you, plans to give you hope and a future." And as a Pastor, it both thrills and humbles me like you cannot imagine, knowing that he comes from my own flock.

Sebastian Young gives his readers a personal glimpse into his own life's experiences, from losing his mother to a brutal murderer as a toddler, being raised by his grandparents, then parenting his own children.

I Had Every Excuse to Fail, But I Chose None

Sebastian K. Young

I Had Every Excuse to Fail, But I Chose None

Copyright © 2011 by Sebastian K. Young

All rights reserved. No part of this book may be reproduced or transmitted in any form or by any means without written permission of the author.

ISBN ISBN 978-0-9826674-0-8

He also shares his professional journey as a successful African American male entrepreneur.

Despite every adversity that the enemy threw his way, Sebastian has used analogies from his grandfather and life's lessons that are embossed in his spirit to help him aspire, dream, and tap into his own inner strength and potential.

"I Had Every Excuse to Fail, but I Chose None" involves the young and the old. It involves our future…it doesn't matter whether you are (e.g., parent, child, educator, business leader) I am sure you will find Sebastian's journey an invigorating breath of fresh air, a reason to celebrate and a call for action in your own life!

Like another proud father in Matthew 3:17, Sebastian, I echo this thought, "This is my Son, whom I love; with him I am well pleased." I trust that you will remember that when the Lord spoke these words to His Son it was only the start of Jesus' ministry and the hard work of calling and teaching the disciples had not yet begun. Likewise, you have only given us a slice of your life but, you are being called to a much greater work that will bring much comfort to others.

Pastor Terrance H. Johnson
Senior Pastor
Higher Dimension Church, Houston, TX

Acknowledgments

It is amazing how therapeutic it is to release your inner-most thoughts on paper. Throughout the course of completing this book, I would start with a simple statement that would spark a memory, which would then evoke an emotion that would take me back to a feeling that I thought was forever forgotten. Although I could have given more, I know that what has been written was exactly what needed to be said. Every recollection in this book is a unique experience that could have beaten me down and kept me down. I had every excuse to fail but because of certain individuals in my life, I chose none!

First and foremost, I want to acknowledge a man that has been with me forever, in fact he knew me and had a plan for me even before I was a thought in my parent's minds; God. You have brought me through and shown me how to make it more times than I can count. It is because of your unyielding grace and abundant mercy that I am here today. Thank you for being my Lord and Savior. It is through your son, Jesus, that I have eternal life.

Mom, our time together was short, but your presence in my life continues today. Thank you for giving me your personality and zest for life. You were my motivation to write this book and you are the driving force that encourages me in most aspects of my life.

To my Grandparents, words cannot completely express my gratitude. Grandpa, your stories are more than words of advice. They are inspirations that have touched more people than you know. My prayer is that through this book, even more people will realize the profound message of your words. You have redirected and led me through so many obstacles with your anecdotal wisdom and timely testimonies of how you made it through your own personal, rough patches. Grandma, I hear the angels singing. You are a true testament of how a wife and mother should be. Thank you for every, meal, bandage, kiss, hug, hello, and good bye that you gave me. I know you gave me everything that you could -- some call me spoiled, but I just say I am abundantly blessed.

To my girls, Jordan, Christian, Asia, and Alaysia. Each one of you is a distinct part of me, and our family as a whole. The world is yours for as long as I can give it to you. I cherish our moments together. I love to see your smiles and enjoy keeping you happy. No one or nothing can destroy my love for each of you. You are all Daddy's angels and the reason I am so passionate about my life. I must leave a legacy for you and I will not stop until I the good Lord brings me home.

To Runday, we made three beautiful children together and with your guidance I know they will be beautiful, strong-minded, and successful women. You're a great mother and cherished friend.

Pastor Terrance and Lady Johnson, you are the head of Higher Dimension Church and God has really given you an awe-inspiring vision. I am thankful that God has aligned me with you to do His work. Thank you for your specific messages that so frequently seem to be tailored for whatever I am going through every Sunday or Wednesday. God is doing great things through our church and I eagerly anticipate his next move of action. Whatever it is, I'm ready with my sleeves rolled up. The legacy we leave for our youth is built with our hands today.

Eudora, you have stuck by through some pretty rough days. I can't promise sunny days every day but I know that the sun feels so much brighter after an evening of hard rain or storms. Thank you for always listening and being a sounding board for all of my ideas. Your words are pure and your love is exciting. You were my friend first and that is the main reason I care so much for you and our relationship. You are the best. Thank you, from the bottom of my heart, thank you.

William Cumby and Ashley Pryor. Thank you for all your hard work and time invested in me. Your input and feedback is invaluable and greatly appreciated.

A special thanks to Vern Goff with Emerald City Communications.

Gary Gerhardt and Joel Turner, you guys have helped me complete my vision. Taking my ideas to fruition through technology, your creative input has taken this project to the next level. Thank you.

Ricky Anderson and Wendell Van Smith, you guys are masters of your craft. Thank you for your words of advice and encouragement. We began this project with a story about my grandfather and a Coke bottle. Now, we have written a book and there is even more on the horizon. We are in this together and we will see how far a story about a shaken soda will take us.

Al Colbert and Ja Ja Ball. The two best cousins a man could ask for. We have been partners for several years and experienced the exponential growth of our companies. Our brotherhood is a lasting relationship that took our family from Beaumont, Texas and carried us around the world. There is a lot of work to be done and we are the men for the job.

Table of Contents

Gertie Lee Young 2

A Living Memory 18

Proving Myself 32

Willie Young, Superhero 54

A Fruitful Unity 70

Life Is A Game Of Chess 79

Talk to the King in the Man 88

Greener Grass? 100

Every Fragrance Is Not For You 104

To Give or not to Give? 110

Forward Thinking 126

FICO 136

Follow Through 143

Greatness 151

Dreams and Destinations 163

Putting Others First 180

Sebastian K. Young

Gertie Lee Young

I Had Every Excuse to Fail, But I Chose None

Every morning that you wake up, you are faced with a new set of challenges and circumstances. Sometimes, yesterday's challenges carry over and greet you as you slam the snooze button, throw back the sheets, and prepare for the day. In certain cases, the same issues that upset you as a youth somehow find a way back into your adult life. Despite your unyielding attempts to bury the past, destructive experiences, traumatic events, and disappointments seem to follow you like a relentless shadow.

I have not had the easiest life. In fact, I have had my fair share of trials. I have seen what it is like to have the world in my hands, and I have witnessed the depths of poverty. Despite it all, I've made it. I had every excuse to fail, but I chose none.

On July 31, 1954, my mother, Gertie Lee Young was born to Willie and Lucy Young in Beaumont, Texas. She was the fourth of eight children; James, Russell, Roslyn, Gertie, Sharon, Willie, Allen, and Robert. My grandfather truly loved her, and although you are technically not supposed to say this - he often referred to her as his favorite.

She had caramel brown skin and stood about 5 feet and 3 inches tall. Gertie had an awesome smile that created deep dimples in both of her cheeks, just like me. My Mom was slender, and very outspoken, Gertie's addictive personality, infectious smile, enthralling stories, and intuitive advice drew people to her like bees to honey. Meticulously neat and creative, Mom carefully tended to her appearance. She hand washed favorite items, and picked up sewing as a hobby so that she could remain fashionable. My mom was unable to afford many of the latest styles, however with time and her trusted sewing machine, Gertie's version was often just as good if not better than the latest couture! She kept her hair relatively short until the afro-style of the late 60's and early 70's became popular. On a good night, she would take her hair dryer and blow her hair out really big and round. She looked like a chocolate version of the popular actress Pam Grier in "Foxy Brown". There was a popular radio station with a dance hall in Beaumont called KJET. Often, you could catch my mom and her sisters, dressed to the nines with their afros high and their feet on the floor of a dance hall in Beaumont.

Being one of eight children provided plenty of opportunity for mischief and fun. My Aunt Sharon told me that one memorable Sunday, she and my mom decided to prepare dinner for their parents. They left church early and came home to prepare Sunday's meal. The plan was to make fried chicken, a vegetable medley, and rolls. They pulled the meat and vegetables out of the refrigerator along with all of the supplies and seasonings. My grandmother's finest china displayed the meal perfectly. Glistening silverware lay on the fresh from the dryer linen table cloth draped across the dining room table. The main course was bronze bird with beads of marinated juices cascading down the sides. The vegetables were a colorful pallet of green peas, orange carrot slices, and white cauliflower next to a pan of warm rolls glistening from melted butter brushed across them. When my grandparents came home, they were surprised and thankful. They sat down to eat and right after the first fork entered the meat, my mom realized something was wrong. The visually faultless meal was flawed! Instead of using flour to fry the chicken, they used powdered milk. Then, instead of a chicken, they accidentally used a hen. While the skin of the hen looked golden brown, the layers beneath were nothing but blackened char. Then, underneath the char was a

5

rare-done bird fresh enough to start clucking. The family laughed hard while my mom and aunt remade the entire dinner.

When my mom was 17, she became pregnant with me. I was born in the evening at Beaumont Baptist Women and Children Hospital. The man that she was dating did not really want to have much to do with my mom or me, so he left before he had the opportunity to know my gender or even my name. At that time, my mother was finishing high school and although she was a teenage mother, she had high aspirations for life. Her caring personality drove her to pursue a career in nursing. Even though my dad had disappeared, she refused to allow her dreams to be stifled. Fueled by her legendary determination, Mom researched a technical school in Dallas and began a grand adventure. Not too many things could stop her from getting what she wanted. When my mom moved to Dallas, it was tough for my grandfather. He loved Mom so much, and her laughter and personality enthralled him. He did not want her to go so far away from home. However, being a true father, he understood, and let her go.

I Had Every Excuse to Fail, But I Chose None

My mom and I lived in a second floor apartment in South Oak Cliff, Texas until 1973 when something completely tragic took place. I was two years old when my mother's life came to an untimely end. Her brutal murder shocked not only our family, but also anyone who had ever met her. But, this was just the beginning of my issues. I will tell you more as you continue to read. Often referred to as the sweetest woman alive, and the most giving, no one could grasp why she was randomly targeted and murdered.

That single incident threw my life into a blender and produced a new beginning.

In 2005, I was driving home on West Belfort when the recurring, but faint, sound of my mother's voice began calling my name.

"Sebastian...Sebastian...Sebastian..."

The barely audible voice coupled with the circumstances of the week entranced me. Suddenly, the sound of my cell phone ringing pulled me from the daze.

"Mr. Young?"

"Yes," I answered.

"Sebastian Young?"

"Yes, who is this?"

"This is Detective Perez with the Dallas Police Department Cold Case Division. I'm calling about your mother, Gertie."

His cold and dry tone made my normal fifteen-minute commute feel like hours. The details of the conversation were overwhelming. In a stupor, I sped through a red light then immediately checked my rearview mirror for police. Instead of seeing the flashing lights of a patrol car, I saw me as a two year old at my mother's funeral. The nightmares that I had long buried away were now a haunting reality. Barely able to give the detective my complete attention, I continued listening.

Although it would take days before I could digest everything that I was told on the phone, the horrid details came flooding back to my memory like a wave a pain…

I Had Every Excuse to Fail, But I Chose None

It was the winter of 1974. In Dallas, South Oak Cliff, my mother, Gertie Lee Young headed to check the mail at our apartment mailbox when a man approached her with a pistol. He forcefully carried her to another set of apartments and up a flight of stairs to a specific door. Standing at the door with the gun thrust into her back, she obeyed his command to knock. The abductor wanted revenge on his ex wife's lover so he used my mother as a diversion to bring him to the door. The sound of her knuckles on the door caused the man inside to inquire about who was there. When the door opened, the kidnapper assaulted the man and took my mother, and his intended victim, to a heavily wooded area. In the woods, the abductor shot both of them, then dug a grave for their bodies. He shot my mother three times, twice in the chest and once in the face. He shot the other individual only once. Confident that they were dead, the abductor stood them in their graves and threw dirt into the hole, burying them only up to their waist. When he was done, he simply walked away. However my mother, being the determined individual she was, was still holding on to life. With everything in her, she dug her hands into the ground and attempted to claw her way out, but it was to no avail.

...so that day on the phone in 2005, I waited for the detective to tell me that the murderer was either dead or on death row. Unfortunately, I found out that he was in prison for a separate crime. Although they had the details of my mom's murder, a flood in the evidence room had destroyed some of the proof needed to convict him. It would be difficult to get a conviction with insufficient evidence.

The circumstances surrounding my mother's death felt as fresh as the morning dew, mostly because so many things had gone unanswered and unresolved, namely convicting the murderer who committed the heinous crime. I could feel my heart pounding and my entire body becoming warm as tears welled up in my eyes. After years of sleepless nights, my family and I were still without a resolution. I tried to lie down and soak it all in, but I knew in my heart that I could not rest, at least not for now. The images that haunted me when I was younger began to replay in my mind. I had to do something to clear my head.

I turned on the shower and let the water stream down my face and body. All I could think about were the corpses that lay half-buried in leaves and other debris in the woods. The images were so real. I felt as if I could reach out and touch my mother's lifeless body. How could he have murdered my mother and buried her alive in a shallow grave? A flurry of questions rushed my mind each time I dreamt about that body with no identity. So many questions loomed about my mom and the man who lost his life alongside her. Were they scared? How did they die? Did someone torture them? Did they beg for their life? Each time I saw the body, I could not resist the urge to reach out to them. I wanted to help them. I became inextricably tied to those images. The souls that lay there seemed to be crying out from that grave, begging me to liberate them.

Both as a teenager and as an adult, I would hear my mother's voice at night. My dreams were pictures that eventually turned into a movie of her death stuck on repeat. As much as I did not want to think about it, my mother's death would periodically reappear in my mind. Were those dreams really her voice? Were those nightly visitations really a sign? Maybe they were a message of some sort.

The call from Detective Perez left me with new questions. In my heart, I did not understand why, but I knew everything would become clear to me...in due time.

Even for the detective, this case seemed to be a long shot, but there was still some small hope that my mother's disappearance and subsequent murder would be solved. As cold cases go, this one would be no different. More than thirty years had passed since my mother was taken captive and viciously murdered. All I ever wanted was for the man, who showed no mercy to my mother, to be brought to justice. At times, I even wanted to do it myself. Although he was in prison for another crime, he was never convicted for my mother's murder.

When my grandparents were informed that my mother had been missing they rushed to Dallas and picked me up. I hugged my grandfather's neck the entire way back to Beaumont. Initially, I was not upset that I was leaving until time passed and I realized that I was never going to see Dallas or my mom again.

My family had my mother's body transported to Beaumont, and we held the funeral at Starlight Baptist church, one of the nicer churches in Beaumont. People wept as they walked by her closed casket. Reverend William McCarty was the officiating minister. Her body had been so mutilated and decomposed that the mortician could not fix her for the viewing. Therefore, my family put a picture of her on top of the casket and laid flowers around it. She had a big beautiful smile and a perfectly round brown afro in the picture. Although I was young, I think I had an idea what was going on. I stared at the picture for a while, all of sudden I jumped out of my grandfather's lap and ran towards the picture. I grabbed it off the coffin and held it tightly to my chest. Everyone took a giant gasp of air. They were shocked! Family members and friends started falling out everywhere crying and yelling. My grandfather allowed me to keep the picture. The emotion of the people made the air thick and their tears fell down their faces like rain.

I vividly remember that my father was not there. He wanted as little to do with me then as he did when he found out my mother was pregnant. My first inclination of who he was took place when I was around 18 years old. I had been dating a girl for some time. One day she invited me to her grandmother's home. We were sitting on the couch just talking and laughing about life. Her sister walked into the room, looked directly at me, and screamed. "I just left you in California!"

We were all confused. I met the girl that I was dating at church and I was sure that I was not a part of her family. Growing up in the small town of Beaumont, everyone knew one another and all of their family members. However all of a sudden, my girlfriend's uncle looked like me and I was getting sick. My girlfriend's sister ran to the phone and called her uncle in California. He claimed to have no recollection of my mother or me.

A few months later, my girlfriend's uncle flew into town to see his mother. Shock overtook me the moment I met my father for the first time, at his mother's house. We had the same striking jaw lines. Nevertheless, instead of talking to me, he referred to me in the third person and barely acknowledged my presence. At times he acted as if I was not standing in the same room. My father maintained the same indifference and apathy about my existence then that he displayed the eighteen years prior to that moment. He did not want anything to do with me. I was left with a new extended family and the eerie reality that I had been dating my first cousin. It is imperative that parents remain cordial. If they cannot be friendly towards each other, they must be present and active in their children's lives. The reunion and connection ended immediately! To this day, I have no real relationship with my father, but I am very close with all of his brothers, sisters, and their children.

My mother would have gladly given her last for someone in need. Yet, someone took her life without remorse or just cause. My feelings of inadequacy as a youth were attributed to her death, but she gave me something I never knew I had. She gave me an unyielding passion to give first and to pursue the best in life. My mother's memory has etched itself into the deepest crevices of my mind. My personality, character, even my physical features are permanent and unmovable fixtures given by her and living through me.

Sebastian K. Young

A Living Memory

I met Runday at an apartment complex on the south end of Beaumont. I was in my early twenties; just enjoying life. On my way out to work or to some activity I saw her sitting near the curb of her apartment. I'd actually noticed her many times before, but I wanted to make sure that I approached her correctly. I planned our first conversation with elaborate detail. I practiced my approach, my first words, and even my triumphant exit from the conversation. It was going to be like a classic love song. I would start easy, make her laugh, and then close on a high note after she gave me her number. The moment we actually spoke, my plan went into action and I was victorious. A smile stretched across my face and created deep dimples as I quietly celebrated obtaining her phone number. We quickly became acquainted and started dating. She had a beautiful daughter, and dreams that I could see us completing together.

Runday's daughter, Jordan, was a little more than one year old when we met. As Runday and I grew closer to each other, I also grew closer to Jordan. She was an amazing little girl that captured my heart with her eyes and softened me with her hugs and kisses. Even though her father was present and active in her life, Jordan quickly broke me in as a second father. We became inseparable. Jordan would not let me out of her sight when I was around and I loved her as if she were my own. On Sunday evenings, we would feed the ducks together and, during the week, we would practice the alphabet and count numbers. My family swiftly embraced Runday and Jordan. I knew that I wanted them in my life forever. After only a year of dating, I had a new wife and daughter.

A short time after we were married, Runday told me that she was pregnant with our first child; I was ecstatic! Jordan was four years old and ready to be a big sister we were ready to have our first child together.

When Christian Denea Young was born, March 18, 1994, it was late in the evening. The entire day's experience had worn me out. As the first half of her body emerged from her mother's open womb, I was shocked. A little queasy by what I was seeing, I blurted out, "EWWWW" and hit the floor. Not long afterwards, my mother's sister, Aunt Sharon, was holding a video camera in one hand and smacking me on the shoulder with the other, all the while fussing at me to get it together before I missed everything.

As the doctor held my daughter in his hands, her hands and fingers made tight little fists. Her legs were pulled in close against her body. A strange black and matted looking substance was all over her face and body in stripes like a zebra. It was scary and cool at the same time. Her skin was a pale yellow and she had a head full of jet black hair, very thick and extremely curly. While lying on the floor for that brief moment, I realized my life was never going to be the same. After I recovered from passing out, the nurse handed Christian to me bundled in a soft pink blanket. I knew I had been given a very special girl and no one was going to take her away from me.

Christian was gorgeous! Despite my hard exterior, the moment I laid eyes on her, I was done. How could this tiny girl make me so weak? I felt as though I had known this person all of my life. It was like the return of a long lost loved one. My new born baby girl was the spitting image of my deceased mother.

After the initial shock of Christian's birth, my time on the floor, and recovery in the waiting room, I remembered a conversation between Runday and me.

It had been earlier in the week and we were in our living room talking about what our lives were going to be like once the baby was born. It seemed as if every dollar I made had a destination. However, I knew that despite my financial situation, I was going to make it work and be the best dad a child could ever ask for.

Growing up I knew what it meant to sacrifice for family and as slim as things were, I was not afraid to tighten the belt and work a little harder. I shifted to my side, looked her in the eyes, and said, "I know I don't have a lot but I am going to get out here and sacrifice for my family."

I wanted my daughter to have the world. I was going to work twice as hard as anyone else to make sure that she had everything she needed or wanted. Looking back, the white men that I saw on television were the only images I had for working that hard. They would spend countless hours working every week. Wealth and success gave them a sense of security. They pushed themselves to the limit and because they were so busy working to build the perfect life, most did not have a life of their own. I was willing to make the same commitment – sacrifice everything, even my life, as long as my family's needs and wants were met.

As Christian got older, we became inseparable. It was as if she was attached to my hip. She motivated me to become more involved in my community. I wanted to do something to improve our community as a better place to live for children and their families. I began promoting concerts, comedy shows and doing community projects. I needed money to provide for my daughter and wanted prestige in my community for creating events and community projects.

My neighbors knew me as the little boy who was always ready to fight and although I could be quiet, I was always up to something. Many of them also knew that I was raised by my grandparents and that my mom had been murdered.

As such, I felt that I needed to prove that despite my childhood, I was going to make a difference in Beaumont. My first event was a concert featuring a local artist. It had nominal financial success but my friends and neighbors saw that I could put together a show unlike anything else that was being produced in our city.

Like her grandmother, by the time Christian was five, she charmed everyone she met. My mother's brother, Robert Young – whom I called Uncle BeBee - suggested I take her to see some of our cousins on the south side of Beaumont. One Thursday afternoon, Uncle BeBee, Christian and I drove to my cousin Margaret's house. My mom and Margaret had grown up together and had gone to the same high school, Charlton Pollard High. The moment she laid eyes on Christian her jaw hit the floor.

After a short uncomfortable silence, Margaret said, "She looks just like your mother!" She then began commenting on how Christians' every feature reminded her of my mom. She was saying things like, "She's yellow, but if she were a little darker she would be your mom." The more Margaret commented on Christian's appearance the more it made me think. It started getting to me. As soon as I got home that afternoon, I took down an old picture of my mother and put it next to Christian. She was right! It was as if the woman that I had only known for two years was back in my life. My mom was present and alive in my daughter's every feature. I was amazed.

Around the time I started to realize Christian looked like my mother, my wife was pregnant with twins. It was an uncomfortable happiness. Although I was making decent money promoting concerts and working for an attorney, I had not yet achieved the career success I desired.

About a year earlier, my cousin Lillian had also gotten pregnant with twins. Lillian already had two children and adding two more would have really given her a full house. Jokingly, I told her that she had more children than the little old woman who lived in a shoe.

Still laughing, I continued making comments. I said that all she needed was a house on the prairie and a white picket fence for all of her kids. So, when she found out my wife was pregnant with twins, she really let me have it. She called me and could barely get out what she had to say because she was laughing so uncontrollably. I think I hit a sore spot when I made fun of her the previous year because although she was laughing, I felt like there something more to that phone call. Pay back!!! When you are from a large family like mine, you never miss an opportunity to laugh or get someone back for laughing at your expense.

Around the time of my wife's second trimester, Uncle BeBee - counting the months - asked, "What would you do if the twins were born on your mother's birthday?" I quickly dismissed his comment and went on with my day. Then my Aunt Sharon approached me and said, "You know it really could happen." Nevertheless, I tried not to think about it.

There were several things going through my mind at this time. Nothing was easy, I did not have any money and I had stress coming from places I had never expected. I felt inadequate. Not only was I making just enough to sustain life with a wife and a toddler, now I was about to add two more children to the mix. I knew better. I was taught, growing up, that in order to just date a woman you had to be able to financially support her, and here I was married with a daughter and two more kids on the way. How was I going to be able to afford this giant family? On top of that, not being able to treat my wife to an occasional expensive dinner or buy her new clothes and jewelry really hurt and now I would have to provide for five people and make sure no one went hungry!

Each morning I had the same routine of getting up, getting dressed, and getting on the road - day in and day out. I had a grey 1994 Cougar with grey cloth interior. It was not pretty but it worked. Three to four days a week, I would make the two-hour drive from Beaumont to Houston where my entertainment office was located. I was researching locations and artists for future events. That drive was plenty enough time to think about my life and the things I could have done differently.

As my mother's birthday approached, so did the potential delivery of my twins. More and more, the two dates seemed to fall in line. I buried myself in work to ease my mind. Engrossed in work and staying busy, I singularly focused on making money. There were people depending on me and I could not slack off or miss any time at work. One afternoon, while sitting on the couch in my living room, Runday burst through the door, explaining that her water had broken during lunch, and she needed to go to the hospital. I cranked up the trusty

Cougar and we were gone. On the way, I called Uncle BeBee and the first thing he said was, "I told you so!" It hit me; today was my mother's birthday! Was it possible my twins were going to be born on my mother's birthday? As time rolled past, it was getting late and the twins had not yet arrived. Midnight was approaching and the gleam of my daughters being born on my mother's birthday was slowly losing it luster.

The contractions were getting closer and I knew the girls were coming soon, but not soon enough for me. All of the nurses were prepping my wife but the doctor was nowhere to be found. Finally, he strolled in and I was tremendously upset. Who was this asshole and why was he taking his time? As the doctor sat there coercing Runday to push, it appeared to me that he was routinely through the motions. Runday was getting very upset. Knowing what a strong-willed and aggressive woman she was, I just could not take the doctor talking crazy to her. Her constant rebuttals to his statements were putting me over the top!

My first little twin girl, Asia, arrived around 10:00 pm on my mom's birthday. However, my excitement was short lived. The doctor was upsetting me so much that I went off. He was taking his time to do everything. When he discovered that my wife was about to deliver the twins, it felt like he moved even slower. On arrival, he meandered into the room as if it was just another day on the golf course. The doctor gradually prepared himself. Leisurely he started working on the delivery. Before he really got going, he was being cordial to everyone and talked to the nurses in the room about random stuff. His tone with me was as if I had never been through a delivery before. Before I realized I said it, I blurted out, "You're pissing me off!" Runday thought I was talking to her but I was actually talking to the doctor. I knew she was in pain and I would have never yelled at her in that situation, however the nurses, thinking I was yelling at my wife, kicked me out of the room.

Walking down the hallway, I kept replaying what happened in my mind. The more I tried to relax the harder it became. After about ten minutes, one of the delivery nurses brought Asia to the viewing room. I stood in front of the viewing room just staring at Asia. All I could think was, if I can't get back in the delivery room to take care of things, they are going to mix my babies up! What if they confused who was born first? Then I said, wait, I can't tell them apart either.

I came to the realization in the midst of my fuming that my little girls were being born on my mother's birthday. They were actually being born on my mom's birthday! My Uncle BeBee was right.

It was nearly midnight when the nurses informed me that Alaysia, my second twin girl, was born. They finally let me back into the room with my wife. I was overjoyed and extremely tired. After allowing Runday a few moments to rest, the nurses brought the twins back into the room. It was early the next day. I was elated. After playing with the babies for a couple hours, I ran to my car and drove around Beaumont telling everyone that our twins had been born on my mom's birthday. I was proud.

Yet the cloud of joy, pride, and excitement that surrounded me slowly began to darken, and I became terrified. How was I going to provide for those two beautiful, but helpless little babies, their mother, and sisters? I was proud to have them but ashamed that I could not take care of them. What a conundrum!

Proving Myself

I Had Every Excuse to Fail, But I Chose None

Growing up with my Grandparents was both adventurous and filled with hard lessons. As I began to mature, I started to realize that my life was very different from the other kids on my street. When dinnertime came, my dad was not the one yelling commands, telling me "Sebastian, you better get home before the streetlights come on." My mom was not the one standing on the porch ready to embrace me as I ran through the door. Instead, I had my grandparents who had become Mom and Dad.

With a rowdy street like mine and creative aunts and uncles, it did not take long for me to develop a nickname. It seemed that I was a quite "regular" child and rarely, if ever, missed an opportunity to release some flatulence or "go number two". Whenever my family would see me coming, they would yell out, "Here comes Stanky!" They called me 'Stank' for short. It was not the most glamorous nickname, but most nicknames are not. I tried hard to abandon this moniker, but it was solidified on one fateful day in the fourth grade.

My grandmother taught me to always respect people in authority. If you ask to go somewhere and you are told "no," then, you accept that answer or wait patiently until you are given permission. My stomach was not feeling well that morning and Granddad had given me something he used to relax his stomach. It kicked in about halfway through the school day! I was sitting in class waving my hand frantically so that my teacher would notice me. Despite my efforts, she would not pay attention to me. I really had to go to the bathroom bad, but I knew I could not move without permission. I was begging to go to the bathroom and she just would not let me go. So, I just went, right there in my pants. It was a gooey mess but I did exactly as I was told.

The teacher was livid and demanded that I leave the room immediately. I was too embarrassed and upset to leave, so I continued to sit there. Eventually, they called my grandparents and adamantly insisted that they come get me. My Uncle BeBee showed up a short time later and carried me out of the classroom. He took me home and cleaned me up. He had his fair share of laughter and jokes that I did not find amusing at the time, but at least I was clean. Although not one of the fondest memories from my childhood, that story has definitely been the source of great laughter and amusement over the years.

I was the youngest in the house, so, of course, I was spoiled. Instead of eating at the table like most people, I decided that I wanted to eat all of my meals while sitting on top of our deep freezer. I would sit on the freezer and enjoy my breakfast, lunch, or dinner with a piece of newspaper underneath me. Why I liked to eat there, I really don't remember, but, if I couldn't eat my meal there, I simply just wouldn't eat!

Money was not a factor for me at my grandparent's house. I got what I wanted and never knew they weren't very well off. Their love for me made up for what they could not do for me financially. Plus, where we grew up, everyone faced the same economic hardships. If one person got something new, we all were impressed and wanted to take part in it.

Even in the midst of all of the love that I received from my grandparents and uncles, I felt inadequate. I always thought that I was less than everyone else was. Although I grew up with my grandparents, they were not my parents. I felt I had to prove myself because the other kids had a different living arrangement than me. Reality and mentality can conflict even in the best environments. As much as I wanted to prove myself, I was the only one who really recognized my efforts. I believe friends, neighbors, and family members witnessed me always standing up for other people, fighting, and being rebellious. But, a lot of my actions were a mask for how upset I was about my mother's death and not having a typical TV home environment.

Almost every activity on my street required group participation. Depending on the distance, we would walk or pile up in a designated vehicle, which was usually the back of a truck. If we were all out playing street football and someone suggested we go to the community pool, we were all going to the pool. No one was supposed to be left behind. Everyone would run home to ask permission. They would ask their parents and I would ask my grandparents. By the time, I had convinced my grandparents to let me go the other kids would already be out of their houses and on their way. I would push my legs as hard as I could to catch up with them, but they would be gone. I felt like the world was punishing me for being the youngest and not having parents.

I Had Every Excuse to Fail, But I Chose None

The simple things that my friends did or did not do because they had parents were magnified in my eyes. I took full advantage of every opportunity I had to retaliate against the guys in my neighborhood for treating their parents poorly. If I was at their house hanging out and overheard them talking back or mumbling about anything their parents told them, I would make a mental bookmark until the time was right to unleash some pain upon them. Sometimes their parents would hear them and sometimes they would not, but I always felt that that was wrong and something needed to be done. I would especially get angry if anyone talked disrespectfully to his or her mother. It would bring me back to the loss of my mother and how I longed to have her around. They were neglecting what I wished for, dreamed of, and desired – a mom at home. Therefore, any game we played – foursquare, dodge ball, basketball, or football – I did whatever I could to hurt them. My mother was gone and they had the audacity to disrespect their mother? It was on!

We had specific rules for street football -- a parked car or a street lamp marked end zones and curbs made sidelines. Although we played two-hand touch, if you caught the ball or were running by a curb near grass, we could tackle. If the grass was a near a drive-way then you just had to be careful. If I heard you saying something to your parents that I did not like, I would wait until the perfect moment. It might be later that day. It might be later that week or month. Either one, I was going to get you and it was going to be when you least expected it. As soon as a street football game started and I knew my target was going to play, I got excited. I would wait for the person who upset me, then follow the ball into their hands. Just as they got near the curb and the driveway, I would run full speed, slam them to the grass, and push them into the drive-way. They were often older than I was and rather than pick fights I would tag them during the game and blame it on the rules. Each time I was successful on my personal retaliation missions, I smiled a little on the inside.

Being crafty at attacking the older boys, and proving myself took a lot of effort. I could not fight everyone and being the youngest on the block I had to make a name for myself. I always had something to prove. Around my fifth grade year, I was really working on my confidence. Every morning my grandfather would give me lunch money and send me to school on

the bus. When I would arrive at school, it was customa-
ry that I would get off the bus and go into the cafeteria
to eat breakfast. There I would wait for the bell to ring
that dismissed us to class. My elementary school was
across the street from the high school. I was going
about my business as usual, getting off the bus and
heading to breakfast in the cafeteria, but this particular
day things did not go as usual. Just as I was about to
enter the cafeteria a couple of the boys from the high
school across the street pulled me in the restroom and
took my lunch money. I was angry!

I had an older cousin, Albert Young, who at-
tended their high school. Convinced that Albert would
have my back, I told him what happened. Because I
was always getting into trouble, he blew me off. That
evening I plotted on how I would get those boys back
for taking my lunch money. I remembered that my
grandfather had a pistol that shot blanks. My mind
raced with ideas of how I would use it if those boys
came back. I snuck to where the pistol was stored and
slipped it into my backpack eagerly anticipating the next
morning. When I caught the bus that next morning, I
said to myself, "If they grab me again, I am going to get
them!"

The bus pulled up in front of the cafeteria. My eyes were scanning for the boys and my mind was strategizing my attack. It was like a scene out of a movie. They came across campus to the playground and saw me walking toward the cafeteria for breakfast. I braced myself as they approached me. They grabbed me and pulled me into the restroom. This was it – I was going to show them not to mess with me!

I showed little resistance as they took me into the restroom. It happened so fast. The high school boys stood back and started demanding my lunch money. I gradually reached for the pistol, pulled it out and started firing. The sound of the gun going off sent echoes everywhere. The boys bolted out of the restroom and left me standing there. Before I had time to deflate my chest and actualize what was going on, the restroom was flooded with officials. The police, the fire department, and every principal and assistant principal in the area were called. The police found the high school boys and brought them to my school. Although I was caught red handed, they needed the boys there to corroborate my part of the story. They pointed me out as if I was the one robbing them. The principal dragged me to his office, pistol in one hand and a handful of my shirt in the other. After sitting in the principal's office and listening to him fuss forever, the police put me in the back of their car and drove me downtown. I was sure they were never going to let me back in school and that my family was going to have to move so I could go to a new school.

The wait at the police station felt like days. When my grandparents finally picked me up, they told me that I had been suspended from school for two weeks. The boys who were stealing my lunch money got a few days detention and were told to never come back on the elementary school campus.

The blank gun incident had greater repercussions than I planned. Not only was I suspended, I had to repeat the fifth grade for missing so much school. I thought I was just protecting myself and proving a point, but not starting junior high with my friends and having to go through fifth grade again was more than enough punishment for me! From that point on, trouble seemed to follow me like a homeless puppy, despite my best efforts to shake it. As much as I wanted to be good, I was usually at the center of most fights, tussles, and arguments. No one was going to tell me how to live and anyone who behaved outside of my rules for living was asking for a reaction from me. Life has rules and in my adolescent world, I was the judge, the jury, and the law.

I had twin cousins in my neighborhood that were a few years older than I named Kenneth and David. They had the fullest mustaches when we were growing up. Their mustaches looked like the type people purchase from a novelty store that comes with the black frame glasses. I always wanted my mustache to grow like theirs, so I asked them to tell me how I could make mine grow, too. Kenneth told me I had to shave my lip so that my pores would open up then put Icy Hot directly on my lip and wait. I shaved my face and put the Icy Hot across my lip just as they told me. After a few moments, my lip felt like it was on fire! It was burning like fire. I was screaming, putting ice on my lip, and doing whatever I could to stop the pain.

Determined to get them back, I conspired a plan for revenge. My great aunt lived next door to my grandmother in a duplex. I waited until the twins had gone to sleep and snuck into their house. Once I got to their room, I tiptoed to their bed and tried not to laugh at my perfect plan for payback. I pulled back their shorts and rubbed Icy Hot on their waists and the inside of their shorts. I then crept back out of the room and ran to my house to wash the Icy Hot off my hands. We did not keep liquid soap, so I had to use the powdered washing detergent.

After my hands were good and clean, I ran down to the park. As I was walking back home, I noticed my grandmother standing on the porch. I blurted out, "I didn't do anything!" Right when I stepped foot on the porch, she grabbed me and said, "Let me smell your hands." She then exclaims, "You smell like Icy Hot and Cheer!" I was busted.

My great aunt made the boys soak in tubs of cold water to deaden the pain. I knew I was going to get it for this one but I could not let them win. My grand-mother fussed and my grandfather gave me his form of punishment.

His punishment came in three stages. First I would receive a whooping, next I was given time to think about what I had done. Thinking involved kneeling on a grain of rice or some type of granule. Finally, we would sit, well…I would try to sit, and we would talk about it. When I questioned my grandfather about my beating, he told me that he understood that I wanted to get them back but I earned that whooping because I was foolish enough to do it.

I was developing a personality on my street as the kid with the short temper that was not afraid of anyone. Still, people were always testing me. One summer, while I was in Junior High, my temper actually scared me. A white kid that lived on Binger Road; the main street leading to our house, had a vendetta against me. He was older than I was and had an older brother. They would tease me whenever they saw me. As bad as I wanted to fight them, I could not fight back because I knew that I could not beat them both. I was fishing in the creek that all of the local boys envisioned filled with piranhas. The water was murky and our giant imaginations often came up with all sorts of stories about what was living beneath the creeks surface. Fishing in the creek was an adventure that yielded limitless possibilities when we cast our line into the water and slowly reeled it in. Nothing scared me so I was always the one to grab my pole, my imagination, and hope for the best. The younger brother saw me fishing at the creek and decided he was going to come down and harass me. I saw him coming from a distance. I demanded, "Leave me alone, or I'm going to get you!" When he got within arm's length of me, he swung at me with all of his might. I dodged his punch and kicked him. He fell into the lake and started screaming about piranhas. I took off running. If he was getting attacked, I wasn't going to be there to witness it and wasn't trying to help my enemy out of the creek.

Later that same day, at the local pool, the boy that fell into the lake was on the diving board. I didn't see any bite marks on him and he was still alive so I figured everything was ok. He got a high bounce off the board and came crashing down into the water. He quickly surfaced and started thrashing around yelling about piranhas again. No one could get to him. He was yelling, waving his arms, and kicking his feet with everything he had. With every yell and motion, he swallowed water. It was only a few moments before all of his action stopped and his body sank. He drowned to death that day.

I got the nickname, "killer" that summer. I was convinced I had scared him to death and decided I was not leaving the porch until school started back again. It mortified me to know that a kid I knew drowned in a pool I was just swimming in and in both circumstances, I couldn't do anything to save him. However, I also realized I could fight and that if your adversary thinks you are crazy you have to use it to your advantage. My fears and strengths became more prevalent to me in the summer months. Each time I got in trouble for fighting or endured long talks from my family my behavior gave me greater insight into who I was and why I did the things that I did.

For a long time, I was not afraid of snakes. If I saw one I would grab its tail swing it over my head and slam its head until it died. One day we were down by the creek jumping from side to side. Just as I was about to cross the creek, a water moccasin slithered across my bare foot – the snake had to be about 6 feet long and black! The feeling petrified me. I made a firm declaration that after that experience, I would never walk in the woods without boots or shoes again. I developed a deep rooted, boot shaking, tree climbing, run for the hills fear of snakes. One crawled by the sink one afternoon while

I Had Every Excuse to Fail, But I Chose None

I was washing dishes for my grandmother and I lost my mind! Soap bubbles went everywhere! I was dropping dishes, yelling, stomping around, waving my hands in the air, and looking for the quickest exit out of the kitchen.

My good friend growing up lived across the street from me. We called him Nine Corners or Professor King Bean because he was smart, but his real nickname was Jack. He lived near my grandparents. There was also a teacher on our street that had a Japanese plumb tree in her backyard.

One day, I was out fishing for crawfish when I heard Jack calling me. He was screaming about a curled snake near him that was ready to attack. I knew the declaration that I had made but this was my friend. I ran to our shed and took my grandfathers gardening tool. My hands were shaking as I raised the tool above my head, swung with all of my might, and chopped the snake's head off. To this day, I do not know how I was able to kill that snake and though I conquered that snake, I still have not conquered my fear.

My ultimate fear of snakes was trumped by my respect for guns the first and last time I shot a man. There was a contemptible looking guy in the neighborhood named Mack that wandered the projects down the street from my home. He was dark, tall, and muscular but he was always on drugs. In the late 70's and early 80's car, batteries and license plates were popular stolen items. You would often see Mack sneaking around looking for something to steal so that later he could pawn the items for money. As I was walking through the projects, I noticed a group of men leaning against a building. One of them took a can and threw it at me. I retaliated by grabbing an empty 40 oz beer bottle and throwing it back at them. The bottle exploded against the wall near them. Mack grabbed me, pushed me against the wall, and smacked me in the head. I felt a knot rise on the right side of my head, so I ran home crying. Uncle BeBee caught me and told me I should not have been messing with them anyway. Extremely angry, I went for my grandfather's gun. It was necessary that I show them I was not going to let them bully me.

I strolled down to the projects with his loaded pistol. This time, I was not firing blanks. I walked right up to Mack and his crew. They said maybe two words before I discharged the first bullet in the chamber of the pistol. POW! I hit him in the leg! My mind was void of all rational thought. All I could do was run. I ran into the woods scared for my life. I shot him at about 7:45 that night. There was a tree house in the woods at the end of our street. I hid in that tree house for what seemed like an eternity. Who knew what Mack would do if he caught me? The darker it got, the more terrified I became. It was dark and I was hearing all kinds of sounds. Every time I heard a leaf crackle, I was sure Mack had found me. The hoots of the owls terrified me. I finally came out of the woods around eleven o'clock that night.

When I reached my house, my grandfather was sitting on the porch just looking over the street. He said, "Boy, what have you done now." He took me to the police station already knowing what had happened. The people in our neighborhood had heard the gun shot. It was loud and they had seen me. At the police station, my grandfather and the chief of police started talking. They were old friends. I was allowed to explain my story to the Chief of Police and he told me we would have to go to the hospital to see Mack in person.

At the hospital, the Chief told Mack that he was going to jail. He said he had a warrant for battery theft and now child endangerment. Then he looked Mack in the eye and said, "Which charge do you want?"

A few weeks later, we were outside playing. We lived on a dead end street, but at the end of the street was a bridge that led to the projects. I knew that if I ever saw Mack coming I would have enough time to run home. I was sitting on the porch with my grandfather one afternoon when Mack walked onto our property. He yelled some disrespectful things to my grandfather and I then murmured, "I'm going to get you." He then stumbled back down the street to his dad's house. The next thing you know, I heard loud gunshots as Mack hit the ground with a loud, hollow thud – his father had shot him. We never learned why, but I was never afraid to play in the street again.

Sundays in Beaumont were exciting for a kid. Everyone went to the local skating rink to, "see and be seen". Around ten o'clock Sunday night, the skating rink turned into a dance that lasted until well past midnight. Sometimes we had a ride to the skating rink and sometimes we didn't. This eventful Sunday, the

50

guys from my neighborhood block did not have a ride and we were going to walk to the rink. We played football all day before deciding to get ready for the skating rink. We went home to shower and get dressed up. The plan was to meet at the first bridge and then walk to the dance.

While sitting on the bridge with our feet dangling off the side and our chests leaning against the rail, we smoked several joints, over the course of an hour. I did not smoke often and even though I tried it for the first time the previous year, I was not a professional. I felt woozy and my head started bobbing from side to side. My friends were ready to go but I knew something was not right. The joints were not laced and this certainly was not my first time getting high, but my body was reacting in a way that I had never felt before. I pleaded for them to leave me behind for a moment so that I could regain my composure. I turned around and placed my back against the rail. As their silhouettes vanished into the night, I laid down on the bridge. I felt like I was spinning, yet knowing I was not moving, I was more confused than ever.

Eventually I got up, crawled to the curb, and gradually stood up to walk. It took me an hour to get home and I was only about seven houses or a block and a half away. All I could think to do was put one foot in front of the other and concentrate. I snuck in the back way to my house. My grandfather was always on the front porch, and I did not want to be caught by him. I made it to my bed and collapsed on top of my sheets. Removing my clothes would have taken too much effort. Everything was continuing to spin. My heart was beating fast. Again, this was not even my first time smoking, so why was my body reacting like this? The only thing I knew to do was pray –

"Please Jesus take this away from me."

I fell asleep and woke up hungrier than a pack of wolves. I thought I was going to die that evening but God stopped my room from spinning and allowed me to live. I never smoked again.

Willie Young, Superhero

Much of who I am can be attributed to how I was raised. As much as I complained about growing up without my biological parents, the morals and values that my grandparents instilled in me are priceless. My Grandfather was too old to catch all of my sneaky ways, but he raised me with his stories. He was a very wise man. They say that experience is the best teacher. I believe that if you have a teacher with a lot of experience then you only have to listen. Many negative experiences in life can be avoided if we would just take time out to listen.

My Grandfather was a peculiar man. Every-thing he did had a purpose. There was a reason for everything, and if you questioned his actions, he had no problem telling you why he did it a particular way. Our family lived in Beaumont because of my grandfather.

Willie Young was born and raised in Campti, Louisiana. As much as he tried to abstain from altercations with anyone, it was a period of overt racism, and people were accused of all sorts of crimes just for being Black. In my Grandfather's late teen years, he got into an altercation with the police from his parish. They accused him of a crime that he had not committed. The police jumped him and proceeded to brutally beat him. After wrestling with them, he escaped and ran. As he broke through wooded terrain over unpaved streets and into swampy fields, tree limbs tore at his clothes and rocks mangled his shoes. He found areas to hide during the day and drove his body to exhaustion sprinting at night. After two days and 181 miles of tireless running, he crossed the border into Texas, and entered the city of Beaumont.

In Beaumont, my Grandfather met the Sheriff and convinced him to hire him. It is ironic how a man running from the law could get a job at a police department in a different state.

My Grandfather always had a way with words, and this chance meeting and his gift of gab saved his life. When the Louisiana police found my grandfather in Texas, fear overtook him. Louisiana was the last place he wanted to return to in view of the police having falsely accused him. The Louisiana deputies walked into the Beaumont Sheriff's office prepared to take him back. However, the Beaumont Sheriff would not let my grandfather go. The Louisiana deputies went home empty handed.

After working for the sheriff for a few years, my grandfather was hired by the Magnolia Refinery which is now Exxon-Mobil. He only made 38 cents an hour, but it was enough for him to start a family.

He was 5'9" with salt and pepper hair. He started graying when he was 30 and never cared enough to do anything about it. He had a medium build and a little gut. My Grandfather always wore a two-pocket shirt. He hid his gin on one side and his snacks on the other - Canadian Club for Grandma and Giblets for him.

My Grandfather's personality met you before he introduced himself to you. Despite his happy exterior, he knew when to get serious and was never afraid to do whatever was necessary to protect his wife, family, or himself. He always said, "I will ask nothing of you but to take care of your children the way I took care of ya'll."

He always carried two pocketknives both very sharp and easily accessible. One distinctive day, he was tested at his job and was ready. My grandfather always knew racism was prevalent on his job and never became too relaxed. He received a new supervisor at the plant and dealt with many racial slurs from him. The supervisor was always telling him how to do his job in a very disrespectful manner. As my grandfather was coming off the crane, he saw his supervisor. He took one of his knives out and dropped it on purpose as he walked pass the supervisor. The supervisor reached down to pick it up. As he got up, he met my grandfather at eye level, and a knife to his neck. Prepared to fire my grandfather, the supervisor quickly reported the incident to other higher ups. They said, "Do not mess with Mr. Willie; he is a quiet man who does his job with no problems." The man had no recourse, and was forced to leave my grandfather alone.

Willie Young, my grandfather was a superhero. He just did not have the costume or a superhero name. He did have a couple of really cool nicknames though; King Cobra and The Black Godfather.

He was a part of a Citizen Band (CB) radio club and had a radio that could pick up people all over the country. Several nights I would stay up all listening to him go back and forth with truckers and other CB users.

Not only was my Grandfather quick with his knives, he was also quick on his feet. I remember several races between my grandfather and his sons. Despite their best efforts, he would always beat them. I even tried to peddle my bike past him. Just when I thought I was out of reach, he would bolt from a complete stop on the porch and catch me by the handle of my bike seat.

My Grandfather Willie did not really give me a choice when it came to his teaching moments. Sometimes they came after a good whooping and other times they took place when he just wanted to talk. He always had a hard lesson and a memorable story to go along with it. Almost all of his stories were told to me on the front porch of our house. He would sit in his chair and I would sit next to him in a chair or on the floorboards. The porch was about twelve feet long, six feet deep, and made completely of wood. There was a small fence that lined the porch but it was just for decoration.

As much as I dismissed what my Grandfather told me when I was younger, there came a point in my life that I decided to pay attention to what my Grandfather was saying. The first time I actually took what my Grandfather was saying to heart, was after a girl on my street and I got into a big argument. He called this his Coke bottle story.

All of the kids on our street were out playing. There was a girl on my street that always had something to say. We insulted each other tirelessly. She would call me names like "ramp head" or "pancake face," and I always had some quick rebuttal. I would make fun of what she had on, her mom, or size. Finally, she started calling me her favorite nickname - Missile Head. I was fed up and started making fun of her house.

The house had termites. Time and weather had beaten it to the point of dilapidation. You could literally punch through a wall in her house with little effort. I told her that her house was like a ginger bread house--then I took a chunk off of it with my bare hand. The kids started laughing and she turned red. The crowd was in my hand so I kept going, "I bet you even have rats at your house that hang from the curtain strings going, AHHHHHHHH, like Tarzan!"

Right when I said that, a giant rat ran across her windowsill. I told everyone to look and burst out laughing. The kids were falling out crying they were laughing so hard. She was terribly angry. I was still laughing hysterically. I could not believe I said it. She was fuming because her feelings were hurt and, without a second thought, she slapped the mess out of me! My face was stinging as my own anger began to rise. Reverting to my Karate class, I tiger fisted her right in the nose and broke it. Blood started gushing from it instantaneously.

My Grandfather charged out of the house with a thick leather cowboy belt and just started beating me in the middle of the street. The pain was excruciating. First, I felt the leather slapping against me then I felt the buckle. It was puncturing my skin and grabbing flesh with each swing. I thought he was trying to kill me. All I did was break her nose with a tiger punch!

He brought me in the house and had me kneel on a grain of rice for fifteen minutes. That is what kids need. First, you have to whoop them, next you need to give them time to think about what they have done, and then you need to have a conversation with them. You cannot do it all at the same time. If you follow those three steps and allow time for conversation, they will know how to adequately correct themselves the next time they get the urge to make that mistake. Most parents try to do all three steps at the same time. If you are whipping them while trying to have a conversation with them, they cannot hear you and they do not have time to think about their decision.

Nevertheless, I was on the floor with rice under my knees when my Grandfather called me for the conversation. I would have rather had ten more minutes on the rice than endure a conversation with my Grandfather. I knew that if I did not answer him appropriately during the conversation then the whole process would start over with another whooping, kneeling on rice, then another conversation.

He told me to get a soda out of the refrigerator and bring it to him. He stopped me while I was getting the soda and said, "Better yet, bring me a Coke bottle." I walked back to him with the bottle in my hand and flippantly began to give it to him. My Grandfather sat up in his chair and said "let me explain something to you." He looked me in the eye and I could smell the menthol cigarettes on his breath. Then, he made a profound statement, "women aren't anything but a bottle of Coke."

I was confused. I knew my grandfather respected women, but how could he talk about them like this. I thought to myself, "Here goes my Grandfather with this nonsense! How can a woman be a bottle of Coke?" I thought.

I did not know it but he was instigating and trying to get me to think. As I was about to hand him the bottle again, he continued to say, "Do you see that bottle in your hand? That is the look and shape of a Black woman. It is curvy just like a Black woman. Look at its color, just like a Black woman."

As he made the different statements, I rotated the bottle in my hands. He then said that when it gets hot outside, it makes you feel cool the same way a black woman makes you feel good. That got my attention. I got ready to open the bottle and he stopped me. He told me, "Instead of opening it, shake it up!" Not wanting to endure another whooping, I followed his directions although I was not sure where he was going with the story.

As I was shaking it up, I was getting upset. I really wanted that soda. He then told me to open it. I told him that there was no way I was going to open that bottle. He questioned me, "Why don't you want to open the bottle?" I told him that if I opened the bottle, it was going to explode everywhere. He exclaimed, "Exactly! Just like a black woman. Now, go put that shaken soda back in the refrigerator and get another one."

I put the shaken Coke back in the refrigerator and grabbed another one thinking that I had heard it all. I turned to go outside. On my way out the door, he stopped me again and told me to shake this bottle but shake it slowly. I started shaking it like before but in slow motion. He then told me to open this bottle.

I opened it expecting nothing to happen. The sound of the carbonation escaping from the bottle as I removed the cap was the only reaction the bottle gave me.

His Coke bottle lesson continued, "Boy, let me explain something to you. Women ain't nothing but a bottle of Coke and you can set the tone to a woman's emotions by the way you treat her. That is what this Coke represents. Whatever you do to this bottle is going to give you a reaction like a woman. Women do not act, they only react to what the man gives them. When you show them love, they are going to show you love. If you shake them up by doing bad things to them like hitting them, they fight back. When you talk crazy to her, she is going to curse you out. Whatever it is you do to a woman, she is going to give you a reaction to complement your actions. That is what women do. Why do you think that little girl slapped you?"

Perplexed, I told him that she must have done it because she did not like my joke.

He shouted, "No! That is not it. It was because of your actions, and how she feels about you. As a man, you set the tone to a woman's emotions. Women do not act - they react and whenever you see a woman going through something, know that a man is somehow involved. Women don't act out for any reason at all; but they are going to react every time."

My Grandfather kept reiterating that a woman is just like a Coke bottle -- you shake her up and rattle the fizz and you are going to get a volatile reaction. However, if you are patient and cautious with the bottle or with your woman by showing her love, you will get an equal reaction.

Back to the bottle that was placed back in the refrigerator before it exploded. That bottle still had a chance. It may have lost some of its strength but it was still good. Some women have been shaken by bad relationships but they are not bad. With the right amount of love and attention, they too are capable of returning the same amount love that they were originally created with.

I now call those circumstances, shaken situations. As women grow up, they experience all types of people, places, and conditions. These variables make up their outlook on life. Often a man or male figure in a woman's life will steer the direction and reaction that women take. A woman's reaction is directly attributed to a man's actions.

If a man comes home with a negative attitude and an angry disposition, he can alter her attitude, even if she is in a good mood when he comes home. When he speaks words of discouragement, she reacts to his statements.

This is a lesson for men and women. Men must comprehend the power that they possess with their attitude, actions, and words. Women must remain cognizant of their surroundings and when they feel themselves reacting to what is being said or done.

The Coke bottle that is cared for will always yield favorable results. When you see that her reactions are starting to become volatile, treat her like the once shaken bottle of Coke. My grandfather would tap the bottle, caress your woman, and put the bottle back in the refrigerator, give her some time to cool off. When you are patient with the bottle, you will get what you are looking for.

When you allow negative occurrences in your life to dictate your decisions, they will cause a volatile reaction. There is a natural and innate desire that everyone possesses; that desire to be accepted. During that search for acceptance, the experiences that a male or female endures shapes how they treat others in their adulthood.

By seeking acceptance, we are expressing our need for love. Based on the level of need, it transpires into the willingness to settle instead of obtaining what is designed specifically for you. Love and genuine compassion for someone that you are dating, engaged to, or married to is more than the big things or the weightless words that people sometimes say. True love is found in the thoughtful actions and deeds that aren't found in books, movies, or pamphlets. Loving someone requires an individual to recognize what truly pleases their mate. It might be a simple task that has been done for years that could be conceived as insignificant but has tremendous results. Take care of your coke bottle. My grandfather wore shirts with two pockets on the front not only for his snacks and cigarettes but also for my grandmother his wife. That is what love is all about!

A Fruitful Unity

Although our relationship had an amazing beginning, unfortunately my marriage did not last forever. Our separation began with constant arguing. I turned to church in search of a solution to the discord in my home. Often I would go to church by myself. Occasionally, Runday and I would go together, but it seemed like when we went to church together, we argued and fussed more than when we skipped. I was working more than ever. My family was just as important as making the money I felt they needed to have a good life. I was sacrificing family time to make money for the family. Assumptions started coming from everywhere.

Runday had lots of questions. She searched tirelessly for answers. My wife was lonely and we were living paycheck to paycheck, but I was working harder than ever. In her mind, the math did not compute.

Runday decided we should separate.

I tried to make it work but it was too late. She was ready to leave and felt she would be better if she moved on. One day, on my way to Houston, I called and said I would move out. She suggested separation but I resolved that we should get the divorce. Even though I was living out of my office and my vehicle, I held onto my drive and passion to always provide for my family. Runday and I are still close although we are not together.

My grandfather would often reference the fact that men and women react according to the actions of another individual usually of the opposite sex. He would also say, "A bad apple ruins a bunch."

I would ask him what he meant when he would tell me to look out for the bad apple in the bunch. His explanation was simple. "Have you ever seen a bunch of ripe apples make a bad apple good?"

He would say that no matter the circumstances, you would never see it. I thought he was teaching me a lesson about apples, but he was really talking about people. In a bunch of apples, that one bad apple in the middle of all of the others will ruin the entire basket. Despite the amount of good apples, they will never turn the bad apples good. The good apples cannot fix the bad apple. I wanted to believe him but the statement did not make sense.

Here is where the difference is discovered. Leaving the entirely ruined apple ruins the bunch, and you lose everything. However, if you take that bad apple out, you save the remaining apples. Similar to removing a cancerous tumor from the body when detected early, eliminating the infection restores the whole body.

In any partnership, friendship, or relation-ship, it is essential that you address potential issues upfront. If you wait until the last minute, the aftermath of a tiny annoyance that has mutated into a five-alarm explosion will be immense. Save everything by destroying anything that could potentially stunt or kill the life of your union. Relationships are more than just male to female in regards to dating, they are paternal, fraternal, sisterly, friendly, and work related.

Take time to deal with your issues, not everything is going to be a quick fix. There are certain items that require more effort than others do. Your effort in fixing or removing issues from your life will directly relate to how long or how effective the results will be.

Look for trends in your relationships. If you constantly experience the same negative results from your relationships despite the removal of the other person, guess what? The problem may be you.

My grandfather told me this story and it makes perfect sense now. He called it generational curses.

In early colonial America, Black men were sold and traded like property. The slave masters would buy a strong man from another slave master. The slave owners only acquired the men to do heavy work on the plantation and to produce other strong men with the women on his plantation. Once he impregnated a woman and she produced a boy, the slave master would remove the man from the plantation and sell him to another slave master. The child is then born without his father and a strong male figure in his life, placing the burden of raising the boy on the mother. She would teach the child to be mentally weak, but physically strong. Training her son not to look at or talk back to the slave masters and protecting him at all costs, often by telling the boy to just do what you are told.

The biological father had no sense of responsibility for the boy; therefore, the boy grew up prepared to do the same thing his father did. That cyclical process continues today. Sadly, we still have black men that will not take responsibility, support, or spend time with his children. Not to mention failing to deposit the wealth of knowledge he has obtained growing up into his child so they can break this generational curse.

As we grow into adults, this generational curse is directly related to our actions. Molested children tend to gravitate toward verbal or physically abusive relationships. They are looking for a father figure or someone to take charge in their life and protect them. This search spills over into their professional life. While attempting to maintain a career, disputes occur with supervisors and bosses. Then they start bouncing from job to job without direction. Through it, all they are searching for someone or something to stabilize them. If she or he cannot find that one to take charge, they find their identity in drugs, sex, or multiple relationships.

The drugs only get them so high but eventually they come down. Sex has strings and exposes the body to harmful diseases. Multiple relationships bring the pain of break ups and short-lived happiness. It is a cyclical curse that has to be broken. No one can survive that way and expect success.

My grandfather absolutely refused to allow his children to perpetuate the dangerous behaviors that stem from generational curses. My grandfather had a hands-on approach to raising his children, my mother, my aunts and uncles, but with me, he poured stories into me that proved to be invaluable life lessons. Those stories have made me the man and father I am today.

Compounded over time, one incident as a child will build into a life of destruction. It is vitally important that men become great fathers and strong mentors. Not every issue can be resolved over night. Your biological composition is completely different from the next person. Take time to deal with your issues and seek professional assistance.

When you consider relationships as a whole, the concept of aligning yourself with the right people can also be transferred to the business world.

Messy people connect with mess. Messy employees have messy job performance.

Chaotic people attract chaotic people. Chaotic businesses produce chaotic results.

Life Is A Game Of Chess

Life is akin to the game of chess. Consider a chessboard and all of its pieces, the strategy and technique necessary to successfully master the game is related to life, business, and basic communication. The king and queen are considered the most important pieces in the game of chess. The point of the game is to systematically trap the opponents king piece. If he cannot escape capture on the next move, the king is said to be in checkmate, and the player that owns that king loses the game. Once the opponent's king is trapped and captured – you have achieved checkmate. The pieces have crowns on them to signify their position.

The king and queen pieces are similar to the owners of the business. They have control of the major decisions and they move in any direction on the board. They have the ability to take that business in the path that best suits their standards, beliefs, or ideas based on previous games or life experiences.

The bishop protects the king and queen. The tip of the bishop chess piece looks like a bishop's mitre or ceremonial headdress. It moves strategically always looking out for the rulers. The king and queen give instruction but the bishop gives advice. The bishop's notes of danger and guidance are like marketing ideas to make the business grow and specific alliances that keep you out of trouble. Then, because of the bishop's efforts and advice, the bishop does not receive payment but receives gifts. A bishop gives the laws of God but in turn, he receives a gift financial or other. Some of us are bishops for friends, children, or even bosses. The job is not always noted but it is always necessary. You want to be the bishop.

Knights are the chess piece with the horse head on them. In business, they are the compliance and human resource departments. When it moves, it can move two squares horizontally and one square vertically, or two squares vertically and one square horizontally. The complete move therefore looks like the letter 'L'. Unlike all other standard chess pieces, the knight can 'jump over' all other pawns and pieces towards its destination. It captures an enemy piece by moving into its square. The knight's ability to 'jump over' other pieces means it is at its most powerful in closed positions. It is good to have people on your team that know how to think under pressure and can come up with quick decisive moves to hurdle you or your company.

A rook looks like a castle tower and moves horizontally or vertically, forward or back, through any number of unoccupied squares. In the beginning of the game, the rooks are undefended by other pieces, but when positioned accurately the rooks can protect each other, and can easily move to threaten the most favorable sections of the board. They are like your sales team that surveys the land and charges forward for you. In general, rooks are stronger than bishops or knights.

Pawns are co-workers or associates that can only move forward and periodically fall out of your life. They are the weakest and most abundant pieces on the chessboard. A small ball on top of the piece signifies their position. Watch your pawns they can be places, things, your friends, or your neighbors. They are your infantry and although they do not have a lot of significant training, they can make significant moves to advance and capture.

If a pawn makes it to the other end of the board it gains power and can become whatever piece it wants. Although it happens rarely, it is an awesome position of change. Some pawns leave work, friend-ships, or relationships and do not make it home from battle – but those who survive, come back stronger than when they went in. You may have pawns that you were not that close to, but after a battle, they can become your best ally.

The queen can move any direction, and can be attacked by any other piece on the board, the bishop can move diagonally, side-to-side, or front to back in order to save the queen. Although the Queen can protect herself, it is the bishop can give guidance.

The wife is the queen.

If you are not the owner (king/queen), you want to be the bishop.

In your household, you want to be a priest, provider, and protector. The man is essentially responsible for these three pieces.

He is the:

Bishop – Priest
Knight – Provider
Rook – Protector

There is a reason there are three game pieces on each side of the king and queen. In order to survive at home, at work, or just in life, you have to be properly armed with the right defenses for successful living. Sometimes your best pieces, employees, and family members are attacked. There has to be a second line of defense for the offense.

With chess and life, you have to see the whole picture. Just like looking at the chessboard from every angle, you must thoroughly examine your personal and professional life now and project how it will be several moves down the line.

Chess is a game of strategy. In life, you play offense and defense. Understand when to back down and when to stand up – when to play aggressively and when to subside.

Your chances of overcoming your opponent, whether difficulties at home, at work, with people, or financially all depend on your strategic approach – how you handle yourself when it is your move and, concurrently, how you respond to the moves of others. Either you will successfully assess every possible move and act accordingly, or you will constantly find yourself in "check."

This is not a concept that is quickly digested. Understanding roles and responsibilities in the home or on the job requires patience. In order to establish roles and responsibility, everyone must be willing to understand that people want to be respected. Often times the way we speak greatly differs from how we act. True harmony can be achieved when verbal communication and physical action are aligned.

I am firm believer that you have to look past the individual and speak to the inherent purpose in a person. They may act a certain way but their purpose and divine destiny will demand a different lifestyle.

Sebastian K. Young

Talk to the King in the Man

In Mark Twain's The Prince and the Pauper, Edward Tudor, a Nobel Prince and Tom Canty, a common boy, trade clothes in order to experience each other's lifestyles. By the end of the story, the characters realize that despite their outward appearance, actions, or facades, nothing could deny who the boys really are. Inside Edward lives the DNA of a King and inside Tom resides great intelligence and a quality heart. We must recognize that there is a King inside of us, and we must begin to speak to one another and ourselves as royalty. This concept is absolutely relatable to the role and relationship between men and women.

Submission is one of the few words that will make the hairs on the back of many women's neck stand up. It is as if someone has called her something outside of the name given to her at birth. In fact, the quickest way to start a debate, a heated conversation, or a downright battle of the minds, is to tell a highly educated, career driven, successful woman that she must submit to her husband. When I think about it, it is like adding vinegar and fire to a science fair volcano stuffed with baking soda and dynamite.

Consider previous generations of women that grew up being nurtured by a grandmother who understood submission - or by a mother who accepted submission. These women would not immediately dismiss the concept of submission. However, present generations have witnessed their dejected mothers struggling to survive without any financial support, or heard degrading stories about men and their inability to support their families. These same little girls from this generation become callous and determine that being successful and independent is their only guarantee that they will enjoy a comfortable and consistent life. Along their journey into womanhood, they deduced true success was independent success. Now, as a woman, respect is demanded and commanded from their peers, colleagues, and management.

This particular type of woman walks into a boardroom and holds her head so high that when she looks up, she envisions a slight fracture in the glass ceiling. She is determined to shatter that glass regardless of the insurmountable amount of pressure it puts on her. Honestly, I do not think that there is anything wrong with pursuing success and removing archaic blockades, but it does not have to be done alone. In fact, it cannot be done alone. I have on numerous occasions either listened to women talk about the problems they have encountered when dealing with men as well as witnessed this parody of failed relationships.

The male/female relationship dynamic supersedes basic dating and spills into overcoming gender obstacles and difficult business relationships.

The Chief Executive Officer, or CEO, is the highest-ranking corporate officer or administrator and is in charge of total management. Additionally the Chief Operating Officer (COO) is responsible for managing the day-to-day activities of the corporation.

In the juxtaposition of CEO by day and COO by night, there lies a dilemma. Women in power positions at work must learn to balance and/or submit when they go home. Women can and should do both – rule in the work place and be supportive and submissive at home. Can a woman's desire to be independent conflict with her ability to speak to the king in her man? In relationships, like team environments in the workplace, if you are part of the team, despite the company or the size of the company, at the end of the day the CEO is accountable for the company's overall success. However, the CEO alone does not accomplish the success. The COO is also pivotal to the company's growth. In the same manner, in a relationship, the CEO, the man, has a right-hand, the COO, a woman. When you think about family and the interaction between man and wife, the man is ultimately responsible for the success of his household.

Imagine if you were at a meeting at work and the CEO and the COO began to argue like two vicious dogs. Each is marking their territory (pointing out their single accomplishments), snarling (belittling), and barking (fussing) to show who is in control. How long do you think it would take for that CEO to become fed up and fire the COO for insubordination? And, as much as the CEO knows he is in charge, he also relies on his Board of Directors (family, friends, and associates), for their opinion. Although the board can be trusted, not all of their advice is trustworthy. They play a role in the hiring and firing even when their input is a detrimental. The water cooler gossip would travel in less time than it would take for you to get back to your desk.

The same concept rings true in relationships between men and women. The man in the relationship is the CEO in charge. He is not looking to be worshipped, but respected. Inside that leader, your boyfriend or husband, is a king.

Women, I implore you to talk to the king in the man and not just the man with whom you are involved. Every man has a king in him, you have to ask yourself, are you talking to the man or are you speaking to the king in the man? If a man has a king in him, all kings demand respect. A woman that had her father in her life had a king in her house and that woman knew that he was the ruler of the home and she respected that he was king. Whatever he said, whether she disagreed or not, was law. She respected his authority as a king and as her father. It is essential that you realize that respect is the most important thing that a woman can give a man. Respect is not blind allegiance to his every demand; it is being honest, upfront, and trusting. This type of male and female respect is reciprocal. Give respect without demanding respect and a mutual level of understanding will naturally occur. Be careful how you speak to a man, once you say it you cannot take it back. If you value him as your king, you would consider what you say and how you say it. If you take, time to evaluate your statements before you release them from your mouth you may be able to avoid many additional confrontations. The tongue holds the ability to empower lives or destroy them. Speak life into him, not death.

Speaking to the king in the man simply means to address the purpose and leadership of your husband, boyfriend, male authority figure, or son in conversation. Women if you talk at a man then, you will get a man that will talk back at you, not to and with you. A man is very giving up front. He will continue giving until he determines whether the woman is sincere or if she is taking advantage of his generosity. That determines what type of man you are going to be with.

Once you see that the man is genuine and you speak to the king in that man, he's going to truly treat you as his queen. With his everything, he is going to take care of you and be all about you.

For this to happen, you first have to give him respect as a king. If an accomplished woman and man love each other dearly, live in a big house, and each makes a lot of money yet every night they are fussing and fighting, why do you think that is? A woman might say, "We don't understand each other".

A man might see it differently. The man believes that they are engaged in a power struggle. A man needs and wants his woman to realize the power he should have as the king of his house and the master of his dwelling. He needs to feel that his opinion matters. He wants the house to understand that his decisions and demands are important. She makes sure that his decisions are ultimately beneficial for the entire family and that his opinion matters in the decision making process. As the king, he desires the final say in the disagreement.

Some women would say he does not need all that power. Oh, but I disagree. He needs to possess that power to ensure him that he is the king of his house. It provides an internal joy and sense of ownership. However, the irony of power is interesting. When a man feels like he is the king of his home, guess what, he will not want all of the power. Men just want women to humble themselves and give it to us first because we are supposed to have it. Then, we will give it right back to you! We really do not want it but we will fight you tooth and nail to get the power. We need to feel like we have authority as king. We want you to entrust us with the responsibility. Now, do you think we really want it? No, we really do not want it at all. It is just a part of respect, and it allows us be the king of our household. Sadly enough, women, you do not have to mean it when you give it over. We are going to give that same power and responsibility right back. Just give it to us first.

Men just want to be king of their home. Although the argument can be over something insignificant, a man will fuss about it just to prove himself or until he gains authority as king of his home. The argument can be made that some men, in the face of altercation, will just leave instead of dealing with confrontation. Although their flight from the situation may be physically or mentally, the root of their dismissal of the situation is their feeling that they do not have control in their home.

Couples argue about money more than anything else. At the end of the day, who ends up paying the bills for the house, the woman, right? As men, we do not want to pay the bills but we want the power and the woman's assurance in us that we are able to handle the load if we must! We enjoy providing for our families by making sure the finances are there. We just do not want to physically pay the bills. Some of us hate paying bills! I hate it with a passion!

This role and responsibility theory is also true in the animal kingdom. Lions are considered to be the king of the jungle. The male lions are large, have full royal manes, and a powerful roar. They also have a unique hunting pattern. The male will run with the pride and live with the pride as a family. However responsibility changes when it is time to find dinner. The dominant lion does not do the hunting. The lionesses are responsible for the hunting. Although the male lion can hunt, he chooses to stay home. Even though he does not hunt he is the chief protector and leader. Each role is important to the future of the pride and is necessary for their survival.

The human male and female were made to have dominion over the earth and its creatures, but not each other. It is a mutual partnership built on respect. A dominant male lion is strong enough to be the hunter and a man is strong enough to pay the bills. A man is also strong enough to rule over his household. We just do not want the responsibility of every task because we are focused on providing income for the family, protecting the family, and pushing the family in the right direction. This concept is difficult for most women to comprehend because they feel power and respect is something that a man has to earn. Respect is, and should always be given to a man. From the first interaction, mutual respect is given and maintained through adequate follow through of male/female roles and responsibilities.

Sebastian K. Young

Greener Grass?

Some women believe that every man is always looking for greener grass. They believe that he is consistently pursuing the next best thing and will never be satisfied at home. However, that is not true. Women often look for Mr. Right Now, but Mr. Right Now does not need you. The guy that you are searching for has already made it and has the things he needs. When a woman comes along and sees a reputable man with everything she is looking for, he is her Mister Right. Unfortunately, that is not what she really needs and that is not who he is either. He is Mister Right Now. He is at his peak, right here and right now. He only needs you for one thing. Do not get me wrong, he wants something from you but he needs nothing from you. If you are the woman that will not do what he wants, he will find a woman that will.

I believe women should look for Mr. Future. Mr. Future has the potential to be successful and has the drive to make it happen. If women would focus on what quality a man has to become successful and then help him to build on that quality, they will grow together. Then, when their relationship turns into a matrimonial union, their future has equity. They may not be financially equal when they meet but the relationship will have been built on more than finances. I know there are some that question if their efforts are worthwhile if he decides to leave before they are married. Your work is not in vain.

Some people are in your life for a reason or a season. Some are there for your victories and some for your purpose. During your time together, you should be maturing mentally and attaining new personal skills as well. It hurts to break up, but when that difficult transition takes place, be sure to leave with something that will help you in the next relationship. Do not drag your baggage to the next guy, but instead carry your accomplishments. Check your RSVP list to see who is on it and why they have made reservations in your life. Build on what you have discovered about yourself and relationships as a whole. Wherever there is a strong man there stands an even stronger woman next to him.

Sebastian K. Young

Every Fragrance Is Not For You

Have you ever smelled a particular fragrance on someone and thought that it was something that you would like to have? You head to a department store and ask the sales associate for the fragrance anticipating how great it was going to smell. Next you spray a little of the cologne or perfume on one of the provided paper sticks and hold it to your nose. It smells great! Then you sprayed some of it on your arm, gave it a little time to aerate, and brought your arm to your face to smell again. This time it does not smell as great. What happened?

Maybe you have walked past someone of the opposite sex and his or her fragrance immediately grabbed your attention. You research the name of the fragrance, and run out to buy get the scent for your significant other. Your spouse or significant other know how excited you were about the smell so they quickly sprayed it all over and stood near you. After a deep breath, you were unimpressed. What happened?

Remember, not all sales are final! You have a 30 day Return Policy but if you open it or let time lapse, you will be stuck with your odor induced headache for longer than you could have ever imagined. Like a migraine, it makes you physically ill, your head hurts, and your stomach aches. All you want to do is turn off the lights, sit in the dark, and go to sleep. But you cannot because the smell is still there, lingering and making you nauseous.

Every person is unique, even down to the way their chemicals react to your pheromones. Certain fragrances do not match certain people. An exclusive, limited edition fragrance is not for everyone and most likely, will not be available to everyone. In the same way, you are an exclusive individual, a special fragrance not made for everyone.

If you are with someone and notice that things are not right, it is because your chemical makeup does not match. You smell good and they smell good, but when the two are put together, it is not as pleasant. Unfortunately, many people attempt to ignore the smell hoping that its presence will decrease with time, only to end up with a terrible headache. You cannot change the way you are made but you can be decisive about what smells good on you. The stress you deal with while around a smell that does not agree with you will leave you looking for a way out.

The other day, I drove by a Kentucky Fried Chicken, and moments later, I passed Popeye's Chicken. They both sell the same thing, chicken, yet, the smell that permeated the air from each restaurant smelled different. Although the product is the same, the recipes are different. The Kentucky Fried Chicken appealed to me more than Popeye's. The initial smell may attract you but once you possess it and commit to ingesting it, the smell and the reaction of your body to the meal could possibly be conflicting. Your body knows what is good and what is bad. Not everything that smells good to you is good for you. Not every fragrance is for you!

Do you know what your fragrance is? Maybe you have gotten so comfortable with your personal fragrance that you have forgotten what it smells like. Maybe you have gotten used to the uncomfortable smell of someone else. Check yourself every now and then. Maybe you need to adjust your attitude, your habits, or the type of fragrance you think is best for you. Never settle for a good relationship only the great ones will last. Negative relationships stink because they are not for you!

My pastor, Terrance Johnson of Higher Dimension Church in Houston, Texas said, "Change the wrapping paper but keep the gift the same." A man is a man and a woman is a woman but if the wrapping paper does not attract you, do not settle, get what was created specifically for you.

Sebastian K. Young

To Give or not to Give?

I Had Every Excuse to Fail, But I Chose None

My Grandfather taught me how to give. In our neighborhood, everyone looked out for everyone else. This obligatory responsibility naturally had its ups its downs. If you got in trouble at one person's house, you paid for it at every house on your street. A whooping was not a gift given only at your own home.

Just the same, if something good happened at someone's house, we all celebrated. Willie Young was a giving man. My grandfather did not have a lot of money, but he always made a way to take care of his family and others.

Albert is one of my favorite cousins. I call him "Man." He was taller than me, really physically cut, and had a fairly dark complexion. When he would get a new shirt for picture day, he would pass it down to me, so that I, too, could be dressed for picture day. I have numerous photo albums filled with old school pictures where either he had on my shirt or I had on his.

Albert's mom was a very beautiful woman who had an unfortunate fall when she was a young child. As she was exiting a school bus, she tripped and hit the ground. Her head struck the pavement and caused brain damage. Although she maintained a certain amount of normalcy, she suffered from unexpected and sometimes violent seizures.

Giving was inherent in my family and done without question. My grandfather taught me that is was good to give without saying a word, or expecting anything in return. After the accident, Man and his mom lived with my grandparents and me. My grandparents never asked for anything in return. Although we were cousins, we grew up like brothers. If you messed with one of us, you'd better be able to handle both of us.

My eyes began to open around the time that I was in elementary school. That was when I started to not only listen but also understand some of my grandfather's words of wisdom.

I received the coolest Batman and Robin Car from my grandfather for Christmas and I was excited. Man and I took my car to our neighbor, Henry Professor King Bean Jackson, or Jack's, house. He showed us his new car also. Jack got the same one but his was the smaller version of mine. Man was rolling my car up and down the driveway. Then on one of his rolls, Jack pushed the car really hard and it rolled down the driveway and into the street. Before I could run out and get it, a car zoomed past and crushed my car under its tires.

Hurt is not even a strong enough word to describe how bad I felt. I ran home crying about my car. We really did not receive gifts Christmas day. It wasn't until after the New Year or later in the year when things went on sale that we got what we truly wanted. That Christmas, all I wanted was a Batman and Robin car and I actually received it on Christmas day! My Grandfather consoled me and showed me that other kids had less than me or nothing at all. I could always get another gift, but that he would never be able to get another Sebastian.

A year passed and it was Christmas again. Children eagerly anticipate Christmas and unwrapping all of their presents. Jack lived at home with only his mother and although she was taking care of him on her own, Jack always had something wrapped just for him.

I begged and begged for a bike that year. My behavior was good for the most part and I had not gotten into any recent trouble so I knew I was going to get it. When Christmas came, I ran into the living room full of excitement and ready to ride down the street on my new bike. When I turned the corner, there it was shining with handlebars, an adjustable seat, two beautiful black wheels, and shiny spokes.

When I went to ride my bike on the street, I noticed that Jack had one too. I knew his mom could not afford to get Jack a bike so I was perplexed. My grandfather pulled me to the side and explained the joy of giving to me.

I was taught that giving could be done in more ways than one. Jack never knew that my family helped to get him the bike but that was inconsequential to his happiness. Not only did my grandfather show me how to give monetarily, he also taught me to give my best at whatever I was doing despite how people treated you or felt about you.

My seventh grade year I observed the greatest act of kindness and giving. It was a Sunday night and my cousins were at the skating rink. I decided to stay home. That year a White couple moved into our neighborhood. They were the only ones on our street and the wife was very prejudiced. Every mean stare or venomous yell told us that she did not care for people that were Black. We could not even walk on their grass. If they saw us on their lawn, they would yell all kinds of stuff at us. I am not sure if it was the cost of living or the proximity to her husband's job that brought them to our neighborhood.

One hot summer afternoon, her husband was out working on his car. I was sitting on the porch with my grandfather. Her husband looked like Archie Bunker's son-in-law from 'All in The Family.' He was very tall and lanky. While working on his car, some ash drifted from his cigarette and landed on his car battery.

There was a loud explosion and a dark cloud of smoke. My grandfather rushed over, grabbed their water hose, and threw the man to the ground. While on the ground, he was dousing the man and washing his eyes out. As water freely fell from the lime green water hose in my grandfather's left hand, my grandfather tried to restrain the wildly active man as he flopped around like a fish out of water gasping for some sort of relief. After that, the couple became a little nicer. It was as if they had discovered some sort of remorse for their prior behavior. My grandfather's quick actions enabled him to save the man's eyes and his life.

How could my Grandfather be so nice to people who were so mean? That thought stuck in my head for days.

One evening as I was lying in my bed trying to fall asleep and I heard a strange noise. I jumped up and looked out the window. There were giant flames down the street. The couple's house was on fire. The husband left earlier in the night and left his wife and baby at home asleep. I put on the first shoes I could find and ran to their house. Without even thinking about it, I kicked in the front door.

The woman came running from behind the house screaming for her baby. She ran into the living room and the house exploded. The thrust from the force threw her into the corner. She hit her head and slumped over. The flames and smoke were now too powerful for me to enter the house. All I could do was helplessly watch as the fire engulfed the house. When the fire department arrived, they pulled the mother and the baby out. She died from the impact of her head against the wall and the baby died from smoke inhalation. It did not matter how mean they had been to me I knew I had to do just as my grandfather had done in that emergency. Unfortunately, I was not successful in saving their lives.

Eventually the house was repaired and a new family moved in. I became friends with the new family but I never went into the living room where I saw the woman die.

I had a lot of graphic experiences growing up. Looking back, had it not been for those experiences and my grandfather's explanations I would have repeated those same experiences with more tragic personal results.

Willie Young was always showing "Man" and me how to fix or repair something. There were many days I had my head under the hood of a vehicle with my grandfather. After a few hours under the hood of my grandfather's car one day, I decided I would go into the kitchen for some water. Man decided he was going to keep working on the car. He reached for the radiator cap and unscrewed it. As the cap left the radiator, a burst of steam shot out from the radiator and melted the skin on Man's face.

If you were to see him today, you would never know that he had such a traumatic accident. After the skin grafts and growing up, there is not a mark on his face. But just the witness of this horrific event made a life changing impact on my life.

I was mortified. As Man screamed, I witnessed a portion of his face fall off like loose leaf paper. My grandparents rushed him to the hospital. The next week, my grandfather asked me to help him repair something on the same car that burned my favorite cousin. I fearfully rejected his request and told him I wanted to be a white-collar man.

My grandfather took what I said to heart and said if that is what I wanted to do then I should start right then. He made me wear suits to school every day. I had to shine my shoes and look the part as if I were going to a corporate job every morning. While I often faced peculiar looks and teasing in school for my attire, this was excellent practice and preparation for the future.

By forcing me to dress up every day and carry myself like a businessman, I learned to give everything to whatever I wanted to do. I knew I did not want to be a blue-collar man. I did not want to sweat outside for a living. I wanted to sit behind a desk and work with my mind and my hands. Therefore, if that was the lifestyle I wanted I had to live it every day in every type of weather and everywhere.

I had to stay in the kitchen with my grandmother because I would not work on cars. That worked to my benefit. I personally believe I make the best bar-b-cue, peach cobbler, and pies in Texas, and like my grandmother, I can cook for the masses.

Many people set a goal in their mind. Once they have what they want figured out, they latch on with the fervency of a pit bull on a fresh piece of delicious meat. My goal was money.

I remember when I was younger I allowed my desire for money to cloud my better judgment. I was walking to school and I noticed three older guys on the second bridge with needles in their arms. They had been shooting heroin and had gotten so high that they passed out under the bridge. I walked over to see them and the needles in their arms. I wanted to watch their eyes and listen to them talk crazy. Knowing they were incoherent, I would dig in their pockets and take their money. Rummaging through their pockets, I found large amounts of money. I was grabbing money as quickly as I could -- not even paying attention to which president was on each bill.

When I made it to class, I decided to count all of the money I had stolen. Flipping through the bills, I noticed a few hundreds, so I got scared and decided to take the long way home. However, that did not stop me. I was excited by how much money I made in only a few moments. I had to do it again.

It was not long before I tried to pick their pockets again. For the next six weeks, I would get money from those guys. Their pockets were like broken ATM machines billowing money from everywhere and I was the only one that knew. One day of pick-pocketing made me $700.00.

Everything was cool until the time I was reaching into one of their pockets and a guy grabbed my arm. It was as if a zombie had returned from the dead and was prepared to kill. As much as I was afraid to walk up on these drugged out men with needles in their arms, I craved the money in their pockets. The day that my arm was grabbed, I got away with such a large amount of money I knew I was wrong. The total was between $1,500 - $1,700 dollars. I always hid the money in a shoebox under my bed. For some reason I assumed no one would think to look for money in a shoebox.

My grandfather knew I had the money stashed in the box under my bed but he did not know where I was getting it. We were sitting on the porch one evening. He asked me if the money came from his pockets. I was scared because it was a lot of money. Occasionally, I would get money from his pockets, but nothing like what I was getting from the guys at the bridge. I was not using the money for anything; I was just letting it stack up. I thought that maybe one day I might need the money for something but I just wasn't quite sure yet.

I told my grandpa that I did not want him to be mad, it did not come from him, and I did not steal from a store. I asked him to wait until the next morning and I would show him. He paused for a moment and then agreed to my request.

The next morning, we walked to the bridge. On the way there, I continued to tell my grandfather how I got the money. We walked beneath the bridge and I showed my grandfather where the drug addicts were laying. Immediately, he grabbed me and turned my face away. One of the people beneath the bridge was my cousin. Out of all of the times I had been down there, which was the first time I saw an individual that I knew.

Regardless of the fact that I was not familiar with the man who was lying there, he was my cousin and now I was robbing from my own family. It didn't bother me to steal from fiends that I didn't know because I knew my family was not like them. Now things were different. My Grandfather didn't have to say much because his eyes said it all. Every time I stole from one of the people under the bridge, I was stealing from someone's family member. Even though I assumed my actions were without consequence, knowing that I could hurt my own family was enough to stop me forever.

After a few moments, my Grandfather asked me to show him where I got the money. I proceeded, picked their pockets, and found about $130.00. I was sure he was going to make me leave the money, but he took it and put it in his pocket. It was as if he was saying, "You are wrong for stealing, but I would rather you take the fiends money than allow them to buy more drugs."

On the way to school, I was happy. I was not hiding anymore. When I got home, my Grandfather returned the money to me and instructed me to put it in my box. I frequently contemplated what I would do once I amassed a certain amount of money. After going to the bridge with my grandfather, I knew what I had to do. A few weeks later, I went to a "rent to own" store and picked out a huge big screen television. The manager knew my family and was shocked when I reached in my pocket and pulled out a giant roll of cash. I paid for the television and told the manager that I wanted them to deliver it that evening. When the truck pulled up, I was down the street playing. I ran home and watched the deliveryman and the manager unload the TV. My grandfather was on the porch smoking. When the deliveryman asked him to sign for the TV, he refused and tried to explain how he did not buy a TV. The deliveryman handed my grandfather his clipboard again and said the TV was paid in full and that someone had bought it for him.

My grandfather was very confused by that point and asked the manager who the person was. The manager, who helped me pick it out, laughed and said, "Stanky bought it."

My grandfather looked at me with almost tears in his eyes and said, "How did you get this TV?" He was lost for words. Willie Young grabbed me, hugged me, and said "You always knew how to take care of me."

I planned to consistently do a lot for my grandparents. I started early by buying my grandfather the largest television in the neighborhood. My grandfather knew where the money came from but we never discussed it or my cousin under the bridge again.

Sebastian K. Young

Forward Thinking

My mother helped to create me, but it was my grandparents who raised me and taught me through stories and life lessons. The bond that my grandparents shared was beyond what people were able to see. They shared an internal soul tie that was unbreakable.

When I became an adult, I watched my Grandparents' health decline. They were in and out of the hospital for one thing or another. My grandmother developed Alzheimer's and was forgetful and often, repeated the strangest things. The night my grandfather passed away, both of my grandparents were in the hospital. They had been admitted for different reasons and thankfully, the hospital made arrangements for them to room together.

When Willie Young died, the nurses pulled a sheet between the beds. His death was a hard pill for me to swallow but I needed to be there for my grandmother. The rest of my family was in the hallway crying. My mind wandered as I sat on the arm of a chair starring at the television. I was shaken from my daze by the sound of my grandmother calling for me, "Stanky...Stanky..."

Her words were soft and barely audible. She continued until I turned around. She whispered, "Stanky…do you hear that…do you hear that…do you hear the angels singing?"

Then she started singing. I was perplexed. My grandfather was dead, what was she hearing? As she was singing, her eyes rolled back into her head and her body fell limp. I jumped up and frantically called for the nurse. She and a team of other nurses rushed into the room and kicked me out. After they were able to get a faint heartbeat, the nurses told us to go home and they would call us if there were any updates.

At home, I pulled out my mom's tattered blue photo album. Flipping through the pages, my eyes fell on a picture of my grandparents holding hands in front of my mom's apartment. At that point, I knew something was going to happen that night. My mother was gone, my grandfather was gone, and my grandmother had slipped away for an hour before they were able to revive her.

Exhausted from the day, I just fell into bed. I tossed and turned but eventually fell asleep. My grandmother came to me in a dream saying, "Stanky, I gotta go, I'm hurting too bad. I gotta go, I love you but I have to go."

Then the voice of my grandfather called out, "Lucy, I'm gonna leave you!" He used to always say that to her on Sundays when we were leaving for church. She would run back in the house several times for some reason or another before we could leave.

Panicked by the dream, I sat up swiftly and turned to sit on the side of the bed. My wife, Runday, woke up and started asking questions. I explained the dream to the best of my ability. The phone rang. It was the hospital calling. Seven hours after my grandfather passed away my grandmother died. I was happy that they were together; upset I was not there, and angry that they were gone.

My family decided to hold the funerals simultaneously with both caskets at the altar. I walked into the church and could barely keep it together. My grandparents were lying there with their caskets open. I walked by them and went to my seat. When it came time for the caskets to be closed a million thoughts ran through my head. I closed my tear-filled eyes and went stiff. The caskets closed and I sank into my seat.

My mom's old tattered photo album has a ripped cloth and leather cover. It is held together with a gold spiral binding. The paper pages have a sticky background to hold the pictures and plastic sheets to cover the pictures. After their death, I would pull the album back out to remember what life was like at my grandparent's home and what my mother was like as a child.

One day, I concluded that although my past had its problems and its tears, I could not live there. I had to move forward. The Apostle Paul wrote in the Bible, "When I was a child, I talked like a child; I thought like a child, I reasoned like a child. When I became a man, I put childish ways behind me" (NIV).

The key word is…. When I discovered who Jesus was personally, I was teenager and my grandfather's stories taught me about responsibility, giving, and relationships. However, the Bible connected my experiences with my destiny when I developed my forward thinking.

I Had Every Excuse to Fail, But I Chose None

I was sixteen, my neighbor called me over, sat me at the kitchen table, and said listen to this song. It was a group that sang a song about a plane crash. The song was like a narrative story. I remember people in the song screaming and crying about how they were going to die. I was scarred and I knew I had to make a change. I didn't want to be like the people in the song. My life could end any day. It wasn't that I was living a destructive lifestyle, but I could die any day and I was not sure what would happen next. I needed a change. Soon I went to her church and joined it. I committed my life to Christ and was determined to live in a new life.

I accepted the fact that my mother was killed when I was very young child and my grandparents had to raise me. I even accepted over time that my father was not there for me. Children need their parents, but God had his hand on me the whole time.

This book is not a biography about my success. It is a tool for personal growth. You can never allow yourself to stop learning. Each day brings new opportunities for learning.

Every time you learn something new you have achieved a certain measure of success. In October of 2007, I was at my pastor's home in Houston, Texas having a conversation with him. He asked me a direct but difficult question, "When did you realize that you were successful?" It was not until he asked me that question that I thought about success for myself. Until then, I never considered it. I could not answer him. That question stuck in my mind for days. Then, it hit me. Success was not a dollar amount it was a state of mind.

Success is peace, its comfortable living, and having the funds to support your needs as well as your wants. Being able to spend time with my daughters and purchase items for them that I was not able to afford or have while I was younger is a great feeling. I did not think I was a success. I was always doing my best to do and get whatever my daughters wanted or needed. Presently, I have been afforded many financial opportunities that allow me to not only provide for my family needs but also give my daughters what they want.

In 2006, I heard Mattress Mack speak. He is a well-accomplished furniture storeowner in Houston. He said, "Successful people do what unsuccessful people want to do – in order to be successful you have to have a passion for it." A light bulb came on for me that day. I was already a success. I had passion, I did what others did not want to do, he was describing me!

In 2007, I went to the Black Enterprise conference with my company in Orlando, Florida. While I was there, I had a conversation with the owner of the magazine, Dr. Earl Graves. I remember him telling me to never allow anyone to dash water on your dreams. He also told me to keep my fire as hot as I could. During one of the conference's events I was able to sit in a VIP section with all of the elites that were there. There were actors, athletes, and giants in the business arena. Sitting in the midst of those people, I felt charged. I knew that one-day people would consider me in that same category. If I continued striving to do better than my last accomplishment and maintained the desire to want more for myself I would be there. I was in VIP and did not realize that I was VIP. Others saw it, but now I needed to truly believe it.

Since my partners, Al Colbert, Ja Ja Ball, and I have been in business, I have gone from organizing small concerts to promoting tours for Fantasia, Kem, Maze Featuring Frankie Beverly, The O'Jays, Gerald Levert, and several stage plays from writers such as David Payton, Je'Caryous Johnson, and Michael Matthews. I have even hosted events with Charlie Wilson, Steve Harvey, D.L. Hughley, Cedric the Entertainer, Monique and Mike Epps.

It is amazing how as soon as you decide to take credit for all of your accomplishments something happens to humble you. We must learn that possessions and accolades are temporary. Remaining appreciative for every gift and compliment that you are given will always provide room for you to receive more. I was raised to be humble and thankful for what I received. It was through a window in my living room that I saw the light.

FICO

In June of 2007, I was living in a townhome in Houston. It was located on the southwest side of town. I was doing well and wanted a home. I went looking at houses that year but did not see anything in particular. I was only half-way looking and figured that I would only move if the house really peaked my interest. After weeks of searching, I saw a foreclosed home, and I was planning to get it on a quick sale. I had my daughters with me when I went to check it out. They liked the house. It was a two-story 3,100 square foot home. I went through the house, took pictures, printed them, and put them on my refrigerator. If I was going to get that house, I had to see it every day and keep it on my mind.

That same year, my daughters and I went to the Houston Livestock Show and Rodeo - a huge carnival, rodeo, and concert held in Houston's Reliant stadium. One of my twins won a little stuffed dog by popping balloons at the carnival and sat it on the dashboard of my truck. She decided to name the dog Fico. I said, "Why fico?" She said, "That is just the name I want to call it!"

Monday, as I was dropping my daughters off at their mother's home in Beaumont, it dawned on me that the dog's name was similar to FICA, the score I would need to purchase my home. Therefore, I used it as a reminder to get my score right so that I could get the house that I wanted. That year, one of the franchisers of my company passed away and prior to the funeral, I was talking to a friend about wanting a house. I was procrastinating meeting with him because I knew that my score was not very good. It was around 623 and I needed to be 650 or above to even get the house.

He told me the only way to get started was to run my credit. I did not want to do it. My friend, the home financer, said the only way to see if he could qualify me was to run it. Later that year, I reluctantly gave him the information he needed. Just giving him the information alone stressed me out. I thought that I was going to pass out in his conference room while waiting on the results. I put my head down and started praying, "Lord you know what I need, and you said you know my score is my enemy and you said that you would make my enemy my foot stool."

The man came back and smiled. He said, "You're good, your score is 666." I was surprised. I told him that number was the mark of the beast and laughed. "Can it go up or down one point, that's not good," I commented. God had made the enemy my footstool and I was about to get my house. I put in a bid on a foreclosed house and waited 6 weeks without an answer. I knew that I would need $10,000 to $15,000 to get the foreclosed house in shape. For some reason they were delaying the process and we were waiting for the bank to approve the loan. A friend asked me to look at a different house on the computer. It was a house in the same neighborhood. My friend said the woman who built this house was a millionaire, and that home was high-quality.

My friend encouraged me to check it out. It was everything I wanted minus double windows. When I met with the woman, she said, "I see what you like but I can help you get the one you really want."

While the realtor was on vacation for the July 4th holiday, I went and looked at the house again with her assistant. After I walked through the house, I went shopping and envisioned how all of my artwork would look in the house. I came back an hour later and said I knew this was the house for me. When the owner returned to town, I told her that I had something to show her. She persisted telling me that this was not the house I wanted because she had a better house on the other side of the neighborhood. I was fixed. This was the house that God had for me. I put in a bid and set up a closing date for July 19th. I knew that I wanted to have the house, move in, and spend the first night there on my mom's birthday, July 31st.

Leading up to July 31st, I worked on curtains, furniture, paintings, and everything to make the house perfect. The owner came back, saw it, and loved it. She wanted to use it as a model. I was sitting in the living room a couple days prior to my mother' birthday watching television, when I saw it. Through the window, I saw a light piercing through my curtains and shining on me. I ran over to the curtains and then looked out the back door. Seeing nothing outside my home, I sat back in my chair. There it was again!

I got my confirmation that this house was made and meant for me. There is something about the way the light from the streetlamp hits my living room window, cuts through my curtains, and lands on the wall. It was cross, a perfect cross. The place was designed for me. I designed the curtains, decorations, and interior colors and had a tailor stitch the fabrics together that I needed.

The first night I stayed in the house, my daughter Christian had a competition in Arlington, Texas, but my twins Asia and Alaysia stayed in the house with me in honor of their grandmother, my mother's birthday and theirs. I woke up early that next morning and was wowed the sun rises directly behind my house now the cross is bigger and brighter than ever. I sat back in my chair to reflect. As I took it all in, I couldn't help but aloud, "Thank you, Lord!"

I look at my mother as my guardian angel, although she is not here, I know that her presence is always around.

The night we stayed at the house, we all slept in my room together and I was at peace. I felt fulfilled – it was one of the best nights of my life.

Follow Through

When you are truly focused on what you are doing and God had His hand on it, don't quit and don't look away. You just might miss the masterpiece that he is creating through you.

The relentless pursuit of your future without full regard to mistakes or hardships is forward thinking. Your past can be a mighty springboard propelling you into new dimensions or a devastating weight that drags you into depression. The choice is up to you. Refuse to dwell on what went wrong or what is going wrong. Instead, focus on what to do next. Spend your energies moving forward toward finding the answer and seeking the correct path for your life.

Success is around the corner. Your assignment in life and your income are directly in line with each other. When you honor God first, you shall receive blessings in all that you do within His will.

It was easy for me to let go of a lot of my insecurities as I grew up. I shed each item that held me back as I learned more about my family background and me. As I continued to piece my life together, I would suffocate one element of my life with other feelings. As

144

much effort as I had put into forgetting the things in my past that hurt me there was something missing. I had to learn to forgive. I would forget certain pains and throw them away but like an active puppy playing catch, my mind would retrieve memories that brought the pain rushing back.

Forgiveness was the key to my freedom. I was devastated by my mother's death. My heart hurt when I thought about being the only kid in my neighborhood without a birth mom. But, my silent cries would never bring my mother back and my angry fits would never punish her murderer for what he had done. I had to forgive him for what he did and forgive myself for taking it out on everyone.

Our fears and anxieties will often drive us to build impenetrable walls that act like blinders deflecting others and preventing us from seeing who surrounds us. Those surrounding individuals could be the keys to our future. I was focused after my grandparent's death but to a fault. I knew what I wanted and what I needed to achieve what I wanted. Unfortunately, in the pursuit of my dreams I closed a lot of people out. When you have blinders on you cannot see anything but what is in front of you. You often go through the motions of life settling for what is offered and never realizing your full potential.

God always finishes what He starts. If you feel abandoned or even stranded, remember to look up and reach out. When He is finished, what you felt like you were lacking will now be in abundance. I often wondered why I worked twice as hard to receive half of what people around me were getting. Although it took years to figure this peculiar equation out, the solution was simple. If I concentrated less on others and their accomplishments and more on my strategies and goals, I would not have even noticed everyone else's situation, and I would recognize the true value in what I'd earned for myself.

As a sports enthusiast, I am a huge fan of track and field. I often see analogies for life in the sport. If I am running the 100-meter dash, then I do not have time to look at what the people around me are doing. By allowing too much time to observe my opponent and not the finish line, I will lose. The next runner is not my opponent. Time is. The goal is to get past the finish line in the shortest amount of time. Maintain your goal and you will win!

One of my favorite Bible stories is about a boy named David. He was the youngest of nine children. In the midst of a war being raged between tribes, David's father sent him to check on three of his brothers who were fighting in the war. When he arrived, David saw a giant threatening to kill the countrymen that he belonged to.

Upset at the idea of his own people cowering at the words of the giant, he was determined to make something happen. With one stone, a sling shot, and divine confidence, David was victorious. That battle was over (1 Samuel 17:49).

Many people are wandering through this world wondering what their purpose is and what specific talent they possess. Your reason for being is built into your genetic makeup and written all over our DNA. In order to find your purpose, you must search deeply within. If you have ever said to yourself, "Something is not right about _____, someone needs to fix it!" Hint! Hint! The repair man/woman is you! Your purpose and opportunity are best friends. What are you going to do when that opportunity and purpose actually meet one another? And how will you ensure that they will work well together?

David saw his opportunity and looked beyond his age, height, or real war experience. It was true that being a Shepherd he faced certain battles. Fighting bears and lions gave David practice, but he had never fought a man this size.

You have probably been practicing your born talent everyday not knowing that one day that simple talent would be the very thing to launch your career. What could you do every day for the rest of your life and be prosperous?

David knew he would receive a financial award for fighting the giant, but he also knew that he possessed a passion for his beliefs and was not afraid to defend them. The bible says that the king gave David his royal armor and attempted to send him into battle. David, knowing that his identity and purpose could only be fulfilled if he were true to himself, takes off the armor and prepares for battle the way he knows how.

It makes sense to follow benchmarks while pursuing what it is that you are passionate about. Follow examples and watch how others have done what you like to do, but never forget that you are an original and no one can do what you do the way you do it.

David stood in front of the giant with a staff in one hand a slingshot in the other and five smooth stones in his Shepherd's bag. The most powerful part of the story is that David allowed the giant to speak and after David says what he has to say, he does not come up with a game plan and walk into battle. He runs into battle at full speed concentrating on nothing else but destroying his target. With one smooth motion, David removes a stone from his bag, mounts it into his sling, and sends the stone flying. It lands directly in the forehead of his opponent killing him.

Giants are only as large as the people who are afraid of them make them out to be. Visualize your giants, mount your sling, maintain your concentration and fulfill the next step in your life's purpose.

Greatness

Most people only take notice of greatness from afar. If the greatest individual to have ever lived were to walk among us, I question how many people would recognize his greatness before it was too late. Webster's Dictionary defines the root word, great, as "markedly superior in character or quality." We will ridicule and take advantage of something great before we give it credit. Because individuals fear being inferior, they will accept mediocrity as normal to prevent anything from being recognized as better than what they can mentally comprehend. So, rather than revere anything better than themselves they pursue complacency.

What is it that encourages people to settle? Why isn't greatness the standard and not the exception? Are we ignoring greatness and stifling creative thought? Shouldn't greatness be the standard that we set for our lives? Greatness is an action!

My grandmother was a great woman. Just like many grandmother's she did what, "Thus saith the Lord." I believe her blind trust in God made her great. By refusing to allow her mind to accept everyday occurrences as coincidence and following the unconventional patterns that the Bible taught her, she experienced a better than average life. Most people walk around simply accepting things and without seeking an explanation or a better more privileged way of living. Do not settle for less – "change your mindset!"

My grandfather told me that the greatest act we can do is give, because that is what God did for us. When a man gives from his heart, God rewards him over and above what we can ask, think, or imagine. When a man gives time to his children, he ensures that his children are blessed.

If people would simply take the time to treat one another like valuable seeds, they would see those seeds grow from good to great and reap a bountiful harvest. The potential of those seeds is locked within the walls of their shells. Only time, love, and patience will break the casing of those seed and produce the pleasant desired result.

This thought came to my mind while having a conversation with James Fortune of the Stellar Award nominated group James Fortune and F.I.YA. I said to James, "You are a great artist. You have two songs that have gone number one in the country, and people around you seemingly don't give you any credit."

My theory was that they just did not recognize it because they could see him whenever they wanted but that they would regret it once the world took notice. He caught me off guard with his reaction. He said, "His worship was for and to God, and that his promotion does not come from people but from God. In God's timing the group's popularity would be known around the world."

Michael Jordan is the greatest player to have ever played the game of basketball yet people around him did not notice his greatness until he was placed in front of the world. Despite being cut from the team when he was in high school, he persevered. In fact, his brother was a better player than he was. Michael used his passion for competition to drive his practice time and influence his actions during game time. His purpose was wrapped in his opportunities to succeed through competition. When you give the world what God has given you then, and only then can you truly change the world.

All of us have something in us that will define who we are. Therefore, we need to use our innate talents fully.

God will put you into something to get something out of you. The reason we have hellish situations is because God wants to take the hell out of you. He wants you to know that it was Him, and Him alone, who got you through. Suffering is seasonal, and I believe, if it's not permanent then it's temporary.

It is becoming increasingly common to see some sort of navigation device in any car you get in. The more you use it, the more you find yourself relying on it. It is an easy device to operate. Once you input your desired destination in your GPS, it will guide you there despite your mistakes and wrong turns. We have to follow our 'life navigation system' so that we are lead to the places we were designed to reach. People fail when they are not moving. Each day that you are alive you must move, try, and strive for your goals. While heading to your purpose you will travel through some tight places and some hot spots that will make you want to grab the wheel. Do not lose sight of your goal or veer off your path. Detours happen. Roadblocks happen.

Stay in communication with your navigation device and focused on your destination, and you will arrive at the correct address He has destined for you and you will be on time. Turn on your air conditioner, follow the path, watch your speed, and trust Him. You will know when it is time to slow down and speed up, but take whatever it is that makes you unique and put it into action. Your confirmation will be seen through the peace you have that everything will work together for your benefit and your vision will be clear as purified water. We will continue the discussion of navigation in the next chapter.

The Navigator Part II

Today's world is driven by technology. With that being said, one can assume that the thrills of road trips have changed overtime. Rarely, will you find a Rand-McNally map folded and crammed in the glove box. Nor will the agent at local Car Rental Company hand you a paper map along with the keys and rental agreement. The reality is that most people who rent vehicles in a city that they are not familiar with opt to pay a little bit more for the navigation system. If you have ever been lost, then you know that the money you spend upfront is well worth it when you consider, the time lost, fuel wasted, and the frustrating circles you could end up driving in if you should lose your bearings.

Like a GPS (global positioning system) to a tourist, a mentor is necessary to a career novice. Just as GPS' are excellent tools for keeping the driver on track, so is a mentor to the novice. Mentors will guide you successfully to your destination. GPS' recalculate when you get off track. From the time of our birth, we have had a guidance system in place whether it was parents or guardians that were placed over us and gave us direction. They are the initial mentors that put us on track for success. Their job is to guide you until you link up the next mentor. God is your forever mentor that you become fully dependent on when you release from your initial caregiver.

If someone has gone where you want to go, why wouldn't you ask him or her for directions in order to get to where they have been? It doesn't hurt to ask.

Greatness is not a foreign concept. However, in order to reach it, I had to consider the way I looked at situations and the way I thought about my inputs and outcomes.

Willie Young used to press into my mind that my subconscious conditioning would always determine my thinking, my thinking would determine my decisions, and my decisions would control my actions. All of this would ultimately determine my outcome.

He would say, "Son, there are four words to remember in life:

1. Awareness - Know where you are at all times and pay attention to your surroundings.

2. Understanding - Always know what you are doing. You will spin your wheels if you do not understand what you are doing. Always listen fully to what someone is telling you and be sure to hear every word so that you do not miss an important part. Then, when you speak, think before you utter a word. Pause and seriously reflect and consider the information for a couple of seconds before responding so that you can take in what is being told to you so that your response is accurate and timely.

3. Disassociation - You must disassociate yourself from negative people and negative conversations. Negative people will always bring you down like crabs in a bucket. Every crab wants to be on top so each of them is doing everything they can to push the next one down. Negativity is everywhere that is why you must make an extensive effort to concentrate on positive experiences and individuals.

4. Reconditioning - The first thing you must do is pray for clarity in your mind and the removal of any negative thoughts. Next, you have to praise God for blessing you with another day of life and then ask Him to open your mind to His ways and open your heart to receive what He has for you.

Your mind is very powerful, the energy generated from your positive thinking and positive relationships will create beneficial results in your life. The process and thinking patterns of successful people can be attributed to how they have conditioned their life.

You may love where you are from, and it can be a large part of you, but it is not who you are. If where you are from makes, defines, or validates yourself worth then you are not living your life. Ultimately, the decision to live in your past or passionately pursue your future is yours. Those past experiences help to develop your personality and decision-making process, but it does not quantify who you are as an individual.

As I experienced everything from death to fires, fights, and family feuds, I could not allow those challenges change who I was destined to be. Sometimes the hardest things to do are to forgive and to forget.

I learned how to forgive as I grew up, but I never learned how to be forgiven. Even though I could forgive people when they would treat me unfairly, I did not comprehend being forgiven. I forgave the girl in the coke bottle story for making fun of me but I had a hard time believing that she accepted my apology for making fun of her. I didn't know if she meant it or not. We have to forgive so that we can truly receive what God has for us. I had been wronged so much in life; however, as much as I have felt wronged, I have done my fair share as well. There are several situations that I have rehearsed over and over again trying to figure what I did to deserve their mistreatment, but I cannot come up with an answer. Then, it came to me. Those negative experiences, although they were designed to break me, I made them the stepping-stone to my future successes. Everything you experience in life is a teachable moment and an opportunity to further refine you. It is not one single moment that gives you the definition. It is the combination of bad days and great triumphs that develop you.

The things I went through and the stories that I was told helped me, and now I want to help you. There are a lot of people who have gone through similar situations as me. You can make it. Turn your mess into your message! I often tell people to - think it before you ink it!

An unknown author wrote, "If you fail to plan, you plan to fail." A great idea is only a thought until it is written down. As you prepare to actualize your plans, take time to consider every aspect. Think it before you ink it. Don't be afraid to take time to learn from your experiences and to think through your next steps in life, but don't sit there forever. Time never stops and neither should your persistence.

Dreams and Destinations

Have you ever taken the time to look as far as you could see in the direction that you were traveling and wondered what was going on beyond what your eyes could see? Beyond the horizon lays your future and the completion of your dreams. No matter how far you go in the direction you are traveling, there is still a point beyond what your eyes can see. The horizon is the range of interest or activity that can be anticipated, but beyond the horizon, beyond the range of perception or experience, is the essence of something that might be attained. Challenge yourself to look beyond the horizon or present knowledge.

Remarkably, your horizon is the break that separates where you are presently from where you can be in the future. There are some who wake each morning, get dressed, and head into the office. They enjoy what they do for the most part, but if you were to ask them about work, most would share with you that "oh, things could be better" or "I just don't understand why they do things the way that they do, I mean, really, it seems so inefficient." What prevents this person from pushing beyond the way things currently are and changing their existing state of living?

People want more for their lives however, they will allow a hiccup in life to retard their progress and stop their mobility. Why be content with the status quos of life?

Starting strong got you on the team, got you into college, or enabled you to open the business that was placed in your heart, but finishing just as strong or stronger is what is most important. The same dedication that you had when you started as when you finish is what makes an All-Star or an Olympiad. It is what separates those who graduate Magna Cum Laude from those who graduate "Thank You Lawd." It is what separates entrepreneurs from business owners. So, take a moment to identify, articulate, and develop a road map for whatever it is that you desire to do. Then do it, and do it better than everyone else does.

The word horizon also relates to how you handle your finances. An investment horizon or time horizon is the expected length of time that a sum of money is invested. The Horizon return is the total return from an investment over a certain time frame. What return do you expect from life?

Understand that your future is yet to be seen and your passion is the fuel that gets you there.

People dream about being successful; however, the dream can often seem to be beyond their reach. Success is obtained through the pursuit of the dream. People will say they are living their dream, but just because they are living a dream does not mean that they need to stop dreaming. Continue pursuing something greater! What is next? How do you motivate yourself to go beyond what your eyes have already seen? Does your dream end or does it continue?

You can reach your initial dreams in whatever field you desire – law, medicine, sports, education, and more. But once you are a part of that profession, where do you go from there? You can be either a generalist or a specialist. A specialist makes the big bucks. A General practitioner can make $150,000 but a Specialist makes $450,000. Are you okay with being a Generalist or do you want to be a Specialist?

McDonald's is the leading global foodservice re-tailer in the world. But the legendary golden arches did not earn worldwide recognition overnight. It took the vision of a multi-mixer salesman named Ray Kroc to see beyond what even Dick and Mac McDonald could see for their mildly successful self-service, drive-in restaurant.

Ray Kroc had a greater vision for the burger-stand even though the McDonald Brothers were content with the level of success they had accomplished. Mr. Kroc, a multi-mixer salesman, went from town to town selling mixers. The Triple Thick Milkshake had just debuted at McDonald's and it quickly became a top seller Kroc noticed that McDonald's was always full of people. Fascinated by the operation, Kroc began talking to them about taking their model nationwide. Dick and Mac saw one location; Kroc saw a franchise.

Ray Kroc started the franchise and replicated the brother's system to near perfection staying consistent with the details and the uniformity that continues to make McDonald's what it is today. Mr. Kroc mastered the duplication process to the very last detail; therefore, if you eat McDonald's in New York and then eat McDonald's in Beaumont Texas it will taste the same. Accomplishing such a task took great dedication. Ray

Kroc was in his fifties when he "saw beyond the horizon," so it is never too late to start.

In business, you have to have a niche that separates you from others. Whatever your niche, specialize in what you do, identify your target market and your target demographic. While you are in the planning process of your future, locate a mentor. A mentor is someone that has been in the direction that you are headed. Then, build an alliance in order to see your vision clearly.

A person who lacks vision or even the pursuit of a dream is like a runner without a destination. Without a specific purpose or goal, the runner is just wasting time and energy. The person may be training for an actual event, but if the event or goal is not known, their training is in vain. Without a clear vision, you are stunting your potential for success.

At some point, you have to take a conscious look at your life. There is a difference between living and surviving. If you continue to work without growth or promotion, there is a possibility that your career is just a job and you are only hustling. Are you in desperate pursuit of your purpose? When you discover your purpose, you will also uncover prosperity, which is the staying power to drive you to never quit.

In life there are starters and benchwarmers, the unique difference between the two is that the starter is determined to not become complacent with their accomplishments. The benchwarmer is just happy being on the team. Starters look forward to becoming All-Stars and Olympiads and will do whatever it takes to sharpen their skill. Benchwarmers eventually get traded or fall off. Are you an All-Star?

Look at Kobe Bryant, Lebron James, Dwyane Wade, Dwight Howard, Shaquille O'Neal, Kendrick Perkins or Michael Jordan, they are all are exceptional athletes and businessmen. The difference between successful people and unsuccessful people is that successful people are willing to do what unsuccessful people are not willing to do. In basketball, these individuals were willing to deny themselves of certain activities in exchange for spending time shooting free throws, jump shots, and three pointers during their free time. They were detailing their craft when no one was paying attention or buying tickets to see them. Countless hours of refining their basketball abilities until the late hours of the night and right back at it in the morning gave them an edge on their competition. They kept their dreams alive by believing in themselves and by pushing their mind and body despite natural ability.

Benchwarmers do just enough to make it and then they settle. They are satisfied because they have made it as far as they have. Benchwarmers are happy to be on the sideline receiving a check for what they love however, lack focus and drive to elevate themselves to the best of their ability.

Being a benchwarmer doesn't happen overnight. Benchwarmers develop their lack of forward motion over time spent looking or living in reverse. Let me explain.

Every vehicle is equipped with three important mirrors, a rear view mirror and two side view mirrors. The rear view mirror is large and used to view everything behind the vehicle. When you look into it, it reflects what can be seen out of the back window. The side view mirrors are attached on the driver and passenger side of the vehicle. They reflect what is coming up on either the driver's side or passenger's side of the vehicle. The driver has to be aware of these mirrors at all times.

The only catch to this scenario is how long the driver allows himself or herself to gaze into these mirrors. If they only look in the rear view mirror, they will never know what is coming up ahead of them or on the sides of them. Focusing on the past prevents you from seeking out your future. You should look back long enough to keep from running into anything or repeating something that you have seen or done before. The side view mirrors are great for changing lanes. But like the rear view mirror, you can't stare too long. Check to see what obstacles or challenges are coming up, but also glance to see when to move or get out of the way. I had to move forward and stop dwelling on my past and although it was difficult, I had some divine assistance.

Priorities provide direction in life. Do not allow your rearview to overtake you. We have to stop being consumed by the rearview mirror; it holds us back from moving forward. Reliving your past is not called living, that's called existing. To get ahead, one must continue to look through the front windshield. It's not only the glass with the widest view; it's the only glass that allows you to see what's in front of you. When you focus on the past, you cannot move forward into your future. Press forward and you will get to the next mile marker of life. That mile marker is the goal that you set for yourself. Just making the team should not be good enough. Ensure that you are not tradable by contributing to the team's overall success, whether it is your company, organization, partnership, church or family. Secure your spot and hold onto it with relentless tenacity. It is imperative that we always approach life with an indispensable mindset. Your windshield is the window to limitless opportunities.

Life's obstacles can create nightmares of a rough past that we tend to reflect upon. The completion of those same obstacles can also become trophies that we longingly stare at. That rollercoaster view of your past is debilitating. You cannot allow those obstacles to become a stumbling block or parking space that kills your career. You have to believe in yourself and abandon everything that is prohibiting you from the continued pursuit of your present or future dreams. The only one who is holding you back is you. Why limit your ability to become great when greatness is fused into every stand of your DNA? While living out your dreams you must continue dreaming and progressing forward. As you get closer to each dream or goal prepare for the next one.

Everyone dreams. Some attain their dreams, some give up on their dreams, and some do not even believe in their dreams. In the end, it is all about the pursuit of those dreams. Your purpose should be the driving force that fuels the fire that inspires the pursuit of your dream. In order to be successful we must have passion, passion is what keeps us shooting for the stars.

When a man gets that special vehicle that he has researched for months, test-drove, and talked about to every person in the barbershop, there is an extreme amount of joy when he finally brings it home. As he walks away from it, he cannot help but look over his shoulder to smile at his accomplishment. When a man witnesses the birth of his child, he goes through that same joy. He carries pictures in his phone, he watches the baby go to sleep, and gets excited when he thinks about the baby at work.

With the car, he thoroughly inspects every button, gauge, and feature. He wants to know how everything works and what he can do to modify and upgrade his prized possession. When the child is born, he checks for ten fingers and ten toes, examines its features to see how much the baby looks like him, and carefully inspects for birthmarks. Both the baby and the vehicle are prized possessions to be admired, but they also require work and patience.

Riding in the car, he learns to observe the dashboard for warning signs and listen for alerts. The dashboard gauges everything from tire pressure to engine temperature and fuel level. The vehicle adjusts itself to him and the way he drives. Raising the child, he learns to listen to alerts of the baby. One cry means feed me, and another will mean change me or I am sleepy. Similar to the car, the child will adjust its temperaments to how it is cared for. The way we handle the vehicle or the child sets them up for sustainability. How long will they last if we mistreat them?

A vehicle that is not properly cared for over an extended period of time will end up at the local repair shop, a child who is mistreated is likely to end up at a repair shop at some point in life. The type of repair needed varies based on the severity of the neglect endured. The repair shop of life could be therapy, rehabilitation, or incarceration. The goal is to fix whatever broke overtime. All hope is not lost for children who lived misguided lives. However, the repairs may be costly in terms of broken relationships, low self-esteem, drug and alcohol abuse, or even criminal behavior. Once the repair is complete, often these children can lead relatively normal, healthy lives. The mitigating factor for troubled or problematic youth and adults is the same - neglect.

As a child, they were led to having a hard heart or even heart problems from living in an abusive home, taking drugs, or bad eating habits. Their behavior will alert others that there is something wrong with their heart. This can put them on a path to having heart failure that subsequently will end their life. Because the brain is sending bad information to the heart, the heart is running hot and is in need of surgery or even a transplant. In juxtaposition, the engine or heart of a vehicle will send information to the dashboard that the car is being mistreated. The dashboard is showing error messages and the engine is at risk for failure. It can break down at any moment because something has gone very wrong.

This heart or engine failure could have been avoided. Take time to pour positive statements into your children and to the people in your sphere of influence. Read their body language watch for alerts and encourage them. Share your stories. Your life is an example. Not every story is a hero message where you did nothing wrong. People need to hear about the bad as well as the good so that they can avoid falling into similar pitfalls. The second way heart failure can be avoided is by placing God first in your life and not allowing the pitfalls in your own life to trip you up so much that you cannot get up. Accept encouragement from others, observe your internal dashboard, which is your heart, if you have become callous to life, take time to soften your heart and experience how much more fulfilling your life will be. Place God in the driver's seat, follow your navigation system, prepare for potholes, and drive into the horizon

Have you ever wondered what motivates Oprah, inspires Ervin Magic Johnson, and enthralls Donald Trump? It is their dreams.

I Had Every Excuse to Fail, But I Chose None

"The biggest adventure you can take is to live the life of your dreams."
- Oprah Winfrey

"You're the only one who can make the difference. Whatever your dream is, go for it."
- Magic Johnson

"Without passion, you don't have energy, without energy you have nothing."
- Donald Trump

What makes them special? We all have a dream, what is yours?

Sebastian K. Young

Putting Others First

I Had Every Excuse to Fail, But I Chose None

I was sitting on my back porch one evening gazing at the moon. I realized that we live as though we are in our own world surviving on our own. But, the reality is that we are sharing this world with so many others, family, friend, and foe. In order to survive in a world that has so many people, we have to get back to community and help make the world we live in a better place for all of us. Just like the lyrics of two popular Michael Jackson records, "You are not alone I am here with you. - Heal the world, make it a better place for you and for me and the entire human race," in order to be great you must serve first.

I cannot say that I have all of the answers or that I have experienced everything that life has to offer. What I can say is that there is one universal teaching tool that transcends age, gender, and generation - a good story with a great life lesson. When we take time to relay the lessons that we have learned through stories with a moral ending lives are changed, destinies are directed, and tragedies are averted.

My grandfather took time to explain life to me through his stories. I am doing the same for my daughters. Even though my grandfather had needs, he made sure his family and I were taken care of first. I have taken on that same philosophy with my family life and my professional life. There is a business term called the Law of Reciprocity. Simply explained, an individual must give in order to receive. However, when you give without concern for what you will receive or how long it will take to get a return on your gift the reward is that much greater when it does come back to you.

Whenever we meet the needs of others, then our needs are met. Holding each other accountable for success is similar to saying, "I am my brother's keeper." Success is built on the accomplishments of predecessors. Like the plastic building blocks that children play with, every successful individual is linked to someone who has done or is doing exactly the same thing that has made them successful.

People are the byproduct of people whom buy products. You cannot become successful by yourself; you need the support of others. We must desire as feverishly for our friends and neighbors to succeed as we do for our favorite sports team.

Putting others first requires one to be selfless. Do you remember a time when you went out of the way for someone and the compassion you felt for that person? It is funny how when we put others first, our reward is even greater that the original sacrifice that was made. Before you have time to count the sacrifice, you have received an increase in your life. God has an independent charge for us. That is "U. S.", a modified acronym for U Serve. In order to become successful, you must serve. We have to serve others first.

The result, or the fruit of your labor, is paramount. If you create quality fruit that is both delightful and desirable, when people partake from it, they will not only be nourished, but they will forever carry a seed from your product with them. If they then cultivate that seed, it will grow and you will reap a bountiful harvest. What is sown into the lives of others is up to you. Whether the opposite individual receives what is sown and allows it to mature is up to them. It is not your responsibility to make sure that each and every seed you sow is received adequately. You are responsible for creating and sowing. There is a certain element of faith and trust in your product that has to take place once you put it out there for others. It is not for everybody, but it is for somebody. Plant in their life and your fruit will multiply a hundred fold.

You have the ability to bring out the best in others. When you notice someone's positive traits, point it out. Your words can revive a dead personality. Pull out what makes them great and they will do the same for others, it does not matter if they give back to you directly.

Continue to encourage others. A common saying is that "iron sharpens iron," but there is a process that we go through to become sharp and it does not happen overnight. You must go through the pain to get to the promise. A great leader walks with their followers and continues to pour into them the dos and don'ts of life while training them methodically. This strategic training creates a template for any one of his or her followers to use once they step into leadership. This is how we leave our legacy. It is not just about our D.N.A.

The time for you to do what you are supposed to be doing with your life is always right now. Everyday provides you the opportunity to showcase your specific talent. Take time to develop your unique gift but do not hide it forever. I was told that the graveyard is the wealthiest place in the world because beyond its gates and beneath the earth in sealed caskets lie dreams that were never fulfilled, songs that were never sung, books that were never written, and business that were never built. Pour your gifts out in words, songs, speaking, or however your gift is to be utilized. Then your gifts are exposed to the world. This is how your legacy is created.

I could have allowed my future to be crushed by allowing the downfalls of my past to suffocate my dreams. My mom was murdered when I was an adolescent, I never developed a real relationship with my father, and my grandparents raised me down the street from the projects. I had every excuse to fail, but I chose none.